THIS IS MY STORY; THIS IS MY SONG:

One Man's Journey
To Turning Oppositions
Into Opportunities
And Fulfilling
His Unique Gifts

Dr. Willie Howard Clemons

Foreword By
Ambassador Andrew Young

ılıı wordeee
where words connect

THIS IS MY STORY; THIS IS MY SONG:

One Man's Journey
To Turning Oppositions
Into Opportunities
And Fulfilling
His Unique Gifts

THIS IS MY STORY; THIS IS MY SONG: One Man's Journey To Turning Oppositions Into Opportunities And Fulfilling His Unique Gifts

First edition

ISBN: 978-1-959811-25-1 Hardcover
ISBN: 978-1-959811-26-8 eBook

Library of Congress Control Number: 2023914054

Cover Design: Christine Paraskevopoulou
Cover Photo: Michael Kinsey
Interior Design: Amit Dey

Website: www.wordeee.com
Twitter: wordeeeupdates
Facebook: facebook.com/wordeee/
e-mail: contact@wordeee.com

Published by Wordeee in the United States, Beacon, New York, 2023

Printed in the USA

Dr. Willie H. Clemons
Photo Credit: Michael Kinsey

"When he came there was no light.
When he left there was no darkness."
—Unknown

"Dr. Clemons is an extraordinary example of grit and grace. Countless people have been the beneficiary of his piercing insights about life, faith, and advocacy. I'm so glad he has distilled parts of his unique journey and wisdom in this important offering."

—The Rt. Reverend Robert C. Wright
Episcopal Bishop of Atlanta

"Dr. Willie Clemons has been learning and teaching for decades. No matter where he lives or works, Clemons engages with the people who are working to make the world a better place for everybody. The lessons he's learned and those he shares in Sarasota, Florida and other communities across the country will serve as guides for all who wish to contribute to a better future for our nation."

—Shirley Franklin
The 58th and First Woman Mayor, City of Atlanta

"A must-read. Not just for young men, but for any individual who wants to move beyond the world we live in today, for a positive impact on the future. This book, because of its practical insights, will especially guide young men on a developmental path that is significant, transformative, and successful."

—Alexis M. Herman
United States 23rd Secretary of Labor

"Dr. Willie Clemons, a Man of all Seasons, shares with us his life's journey in this book, *This Is My Story; This Is My Song*. He demonstrates a dedicated life of service designed to impact others. This book captures the true essence of giving and mentorship for those who wish to follow and those yet to come. A must read that provides a blueprint that will motivate and guide us to fulfilling our dreams and goals."

—Charles Teamer, Past Grand Sire Archon
Sigma Pi Phi Fraternity (Boule) and
the 27th General President,
Alpha Phi Alpha Fraternity.

"Dr. Willie Clemons created the fabric of Atlanta with his creativity, his imaginative goals and programmatic thrusts for Atlantans to enjoy and participate in the success of the beloved community."

—Xernona Clayton
Creator of the Trumpet Awards

"Over the years of family and friendship, Henry and I watched with amazement Dr. Willie Clemons engaging in public service in Atlanta. His commitment to mentoring and volunteering for charitable and human rights causes are priceless. As a trailblazer, whose mission is to "strengthen our community by helping those in need," he has left an indelible mark for our generation and those yet to come. This book tells how he did it."

—Mrs. Billye Suber Aaron
and in Memory of Henry "Hank" Aaron

"Dr. Clemons gives invaluable lessons for the next generation of leaders with a captivating blend of history, inspiration, and wisdom. This book is an empowering testament to the impact that can be achieved through unity and purpose. A must-read for those seeking to understand how to effect change and leave a lasting legacy of positive influence."

—Derek 'Fonzworth Bentley' Watkins
Entertainer

"From his first ones in Mobile, Alabama to those in Atlanta and ultimately to Sarasota, Florida, the steps of Dr. Willie Clemons have been ordered by God. And through his remarkable life journey, he was molded and shaped by historic change-makers who inspired his purpose-driven life for the betterment of others. These pages document for generations yet to come, the story of how an ordinary soul can make an extraordinary impact across the space he travels in this life."

—U. S. Congressman Sanford D. Bishop, Jr.

"Over the years, Dr. Willie Clemons has had a strong commitment to leadership and to mentoring young people. Many individuals have benefited from his wisdom, his commitment, and his enthusiasm for serving others."

—Louis W. Sullivan, M.D.
U.S. Secretary of Health and Human Services, 1989-1993
Founding President, Morehouse School of Medicine

N ow more than ever, in a world turned upside down, we feel there is a need for the kind of inspiration, wisdom, guidance and leadership Dr. Willie Clemons shares with us in his book *THIS IS MY STORY; THIS IS MY SONG: One Man's Journey To Turning Oppositions Into Opportunities And Fulfilling His Unique Gifts*.

Fifty years ago, I had the pleasure of meeting Dr. Clemons and family upon his arrival in Atlanta to open Atlanta Junior College with my late wife Jean. This was a continuation of his lifelong journey to "strengthen our community and help those in need." In doing his part as a public servant and legacy holder, he embarked upon a project that needed to be published and shared with others. Dr. Clemons is writing a book that can be impactful to those who need it. For many, fortitude and life choices are often influenced in the home but for many more, there is no guiding light to their NorthStar. *THIS IS MY STORY; THIS IS MY SONG: One Man's Journey To Turning Oppositions Into Opportunities And Fulfilling His Unique Gifts* is a guiding light and has universal appeal for those in service to others, a cause he has dedicated his life to with stellar results. Dr. Clemons dream is that this book will serve as a mentorship guide for those who need someone to hold their space. He also hopes that this book will inspire and motivate readers to live energetically, fearlessly, embrace all that life offers and feverishly move toward the vision they hold for their unique lives, in turn passing it on to future generations.

The book begins in Mobile, Alabama where he was born and takes us through his journey of becoming a significant influencer and activist of change. Through his dynamic years in Atlanta where his role, along with the great men and women heralding change for the betterment of people of color and beyond, and finally through to his move to Sarasota, Florida. Along the way we meet a plethora of some of the greatest people who ever lived.

But this book is not just an inspirational story of a man who has fully embraced life and his people or about effecting massive change with the powerful people who became a part of his circle, it is truly unique. Unique to this book are the teachable moments he leaves behind for the young men who desire to walk a similar path in life. Understanding and encouraging, it is a seminal work on how change happens and the solidarity of mind spirit and community it takes to achieve such success. This is a must read. Please enjoy.

Peace and Blessings,

Andrew Young

DEDICATION

This book is dedicated to a group of phenomenal women and the courageous men in my life. My unsung heroines and heroes. My wife and best friend, Leteria Seals Clemons, who has been my rock, partner, and foundation of our family. She is the gift from God and is truly the "best thing that ever happened to me." Daughters Lybra and Lailee Clemons, two amazing and accomplished women. I am so proud to be your father and to be called "Daddy" by you. You bring love and happiness to me and our family.

My mother Mabel Williams, who loved and supported me unconditionally, my Aunts, Catherine Todd Washington (godmother), Maggie Todd Singleton, Alma Todd Brown, and mother-in law Edna Seals. My grandfather and role model, Will Todd, grandmother, Arcola Robinson Todd, stepfather Roger Williams, father-in-law Frank Seals, mentor Dr. Gaines Thompson, cousins Marva Henry Watkins and Helen Singleton Kirk, friend Vincent Warren Henderson and my special advisor, Laurent Delly.

"The standards of the civilization into which you are born are first outside of you, and by the time you get to be a man they're inside of you."

—James Baldwin

TABLE OF CONTENTS

AUTHOR'S NOTE

"To whom much is given, much is required."

—Luke 12:48

This book offers a roadmap to success one could pick up, relate to, and say, "Hey, I've struggled with similar issues, concerns, and challenges in my life. And I can now relate as someone who can offer guidance and an approach to getting through it all." If your aspirations in life are aligned with what mine are and have been, then this is a road map in helping you navigate your journey. The foundation of this blueprint is a combination of solid family values and practical steps that you can leverage into meaningful action.

With a heart for service and the strength drawn from biblical principles, I firmly believe in the powerful words found in Luke 12:48. "To whom much is given, much is required." The unique gifts I have been given have led me into a life of service, and it is in this spirit of service that compels me to share my experiences. So, if you wish to leverage your unique talents and gifts to having a powerful impact in this world, this book can serve as a blueprint to explore your calling; and I pray it meets you where you are and are meant to be.

Your actions matter! They matter when they take place locally— within your community and family, for example. But they also matter when applied to a broader platform such as in the political and business arena. Now more than ever, the need for Black voices in conversations at all levels is critical, as is our participation to offer meaningful solutions and lobby for the equity and social justice in our communities.

Unfortunately, we are not living in an equitable society in America—or in the world for that matter. So, our voices are not included within the most critical conversations that impact our lives, and especially our future. Our voices must be clear, sound, and our actions must be decisive. Only then will we be given a platform to share the value of what we can bring to the table. I have a voice. As a Black man in the United States, I have found that my personal success has been amplified due to the access to power brokers to HEAR and receive my voice and message. Success brings access!

Throughout my life I have been fortunate enough to help others create their roadmaps for success despite living in a country insensitive to their needs. And so, I offer my perspective, my expertise, successful strategies, and lessons learned—for my community.

For me, it all began with my family, as it does for most people. I was blessed to have been raised and guided by a spiritual family which was typical of many African Americans who grew up in Mobile, Alabama. For a great many centuries, our spiritual connection was the only thing in our lives that was not co-opted or dictated by someone else. Our faith was the only thing we could do independently of another's approval, and it became an important part of the root of Black identity. The church was therefore cherished, and an intricate part of Black life.

The Power of Faith Can Move Mountains, But Some Mountains Take Longer to Move Than Others.

In many ways, we are still captives to our slave masters. This, despite our constitutional freedom. I speak now of what is happening with our family value systems, our declining graduation rates, our higher education aspirations, and our exclusion and marginalization in the political arena and in corporate America.

We must understand that translating constitutional freedom and equality into a societal reality will happen only by our own efforts derived out of the ashes of slavery. Freedom, equality, and equity is our constitutional right, and it is through our own efforts that we will claim them. As African Americans, we are a resilient group, and we now have a chance to use our resiliency to create and make positive changes for our race. Whether it is in politics or at the helm of corporations, in pulpits or classrooms, to rebuild a solid family should be our aim and in so doing, we will be poised to step into our own greatness.

We have endured over four hundred years of institutional racism, and that has left us with where we are now. In 2018, I read an article in *The Nation* that stated it would take the average Black family 228 years to build the wealth of a white family today. As African Americans, we have not been given the same chance to be in ultimate control of our destinies. Although some would argue differently. But in my opinion, we will never be fully in control of our destiny until the playing field is level. However, there are myriad things we can do to help level that field. Fieldwork is something we know, for we have tilled, planted, and harvested it, and we will level it and reap it. Now, it is time to collect on the fruits of our labor.

Our lives as Black folks in the world have been tainted by misinformation, propaganda, and skewed marketing which has adversely affected our lives. As the wealth creators of the world, it was in the best interests of our oppressors to dictate our lives, especially since we were considered less than two-thirds of a human being. We were told what we could own, where we could live, what we were capable of doing and in so many insidious ways we are still being marginalized. Their goals have always been to keep us in our place and to subdue uprisings. During slavery, the tactics were fear mongering, lynchings, whippings, rape, and every heinous thing under the sun. Today, Black communities are stifled by drug problems, alcohol abuse, school dropouts, wide-spread poverty, single parent families, and violent crime. These problems did not spring out of thin air. They are tactical elements in a war still being waged against us, and they have successfully led our communities away from the paths of education, free-thinking, and problem-solving. Most certainly our stations in life as rulers and warriors before coming to this foreign land was quelled by the harsh reality of slavery but the dignity, spirit and wisdom of our ancestors still lives within us.

When we have dared to push back against these thinly veiled atrocities that have led our communities astray, we are mercilessly reminded to stay in our place. Using poverty as a political construct and money as seduction leads many to blindly follow the road to nowhere.

We may no longer live in the age of church Sundays, but we must find a way to lead our young people to higher ground. If nothing else, we must re-introduce the tradition of spiritually grounding our families to our communities, for faith unseen is in the heart of every man. To effect sustainable change in our communities, we must know and believe that faith can indeed move mountains. If you act and achieve in such a way that brings honor to God, you will naturally be lifting up those around you too.

An intense focus on individualism over community and materialism over spirituality are two of the biggest issues the Black community faces in the US today. No longer do we hold the biblical principle to "Love thy neighbor as thyself" (Mark 12:31). The moment we reconnect these dots and engage our financial acumen, I believe our battle will be won.

Never should we undervalue the need to do what is right and just. In my life, these principles were pivotal in finding my worth and success in life. I've recognized my mission and like to think I've done things that have offered a tremendous impact on Black children who may otherwise have been lost, as well as on adults who needed a mentor's wisdom to recognize their own greatness.

There is an impressive list of Black people who are high achievers, but there are far more who suffer the psychological scars of our history. Post Traumatic Slave Disorder (PTSD) has had an enormous effect on who we believe we are and the decisions we make. In her book, *Post Traumatic Slave Syndrome*, Dr. Joy DeGruy Leary describes this PTSD as a mental health condition that is triggered by a terrifying event—either experienced or witnessed. Mentally we are enslaved by something we cannot see and that is not easy to define. Consider the former slave master from the British West Indies who gave this speech in Virginia dubbed the Willie Lynch letters. In it he suggested that a far more effective method of control than corporal punishment was to control the psychological state of slaves by pitting them against each other. "This method," he assured his audience, "will control the slaves for at least three hundred years." Gone may be the days of a lynching with a rope. This has been replaced with something even more lethal, a high-tech lynching that is both electronic and psychological in nature.

We are at a pivotal moment where it is time, as the erudite Bob Marley wrote, "to emancipate yourselves from mental slavery." It is time to identify what makes us unique as a people. Managing our collective trauma is something we could learn from the Jewish community. Jewish communities in America have managed to memorialize their collective trauma from the Holocaust in a way that inspires their progeny to take charge of their lives and future by understanding their drive to engage in the world of business and finance successfully. Today, the Jewish people are some of the richest Americans, and some would argue that they run both Wall Street and Hollywood, two of America's most celebrated industries.

How did they play the game? How did they get to checkmate and therefore perceived equality? How can the Black community position our gifts so that they can make a difference in our collective and individual lives? I am enormously blessed to be one of a group of Black leaders who make it their lifelong mission to motivate our people to lay down their burdens, to climb all the way up to their NorthStar, and in turn help others to do the same. My mission is to help you find your way to your personal best, in difficult circumstances. One of the ways I can do that is to offer insights into how the system works against us. I write this book from the perspective of one man who has been blessed to have had a seat at the table with knowledge to share with you.

The system may feel like it's against you at times; however, it should never feel like you cannot conquer it. Soldier on. If you feel like a second-class citizen, and if you accept that premise to be true, you'll be treated like one. If you know you are an equal and act as such, your voice will be heard. I am here to help develop voices of clarity, reason, and compromise, so that we can bring change to our communities.

This can feel overwhelming, even daunting. I used to feel that success was an insurmountable obstacle, but I don't feel that way anymore. I did the work and because of where I am today I am secure in the confidence that comes from the experience of doing it. My concern is for those who have been left behind—those swimming upstream against a strong current. How can I help my people grow into their own success, and overcome the restrictions put upon them by fear and by race? What can I do to help support my community so that they have the appropriate tools for them to reach the apex of their potential—and do this by leveraging their unique skills and talents? This is MY mission, my aspiration, my purpose, and my divine calling, 'til my last breath is drawn.

So, you see, this is why I use my voice to empower others. This is my reason for helping countless numbers of people, equipping them with the tools to deal with their inner demons that can spiral them downward, ultimately leading them astray. If I have been helpful to you at any point in your life to achieve the success that you have always wanted, I strongly encourage you to keep this chain going and open your heart and reach out to those in need. Treat others with dignity and respect and above all, extend as much of a helping hand as your resources allow.

There are many powerful personal testimonies by accomplished Black men and women in this world. But seldom are they published. It is my deep hope that in this book you might find the inspiration to claim your rightful place in this world. It is time to change your perspective. It is time to seize the opportunities that will help you thrive personally. It is time to add your successes to the collective community. And, it is time for us to inhabit our heritage of greatness and become a fully actualized people in these United States of America.

Unique and blessed,
Willie Howard Clemons

CHAPTER ONE

RAISED ON LOVE

Our family is a circle of strength and love.... Our family
with every birth and every union the circle grows, our family
is a circle of strength every crisis faced together
makes the circle stronger.

—Harriet Morgan

It's quite likely that a child comes into the world with a pre-ordained purpose. For me it seemed that way. From a very early age I was sure of my purpose and never doubted that I was born to be of service to others. Whether this overarching purpose was innate or learned from my Papa, whose life was dedicated to change, my relentless grandmother who instilled in me the need to rise above my circumstances, the church that emphasized a giving spirit, or directly from God, I am a firm believer that a life well lived is noted by the difference you make in other people's lives. To this day, it is my driving force. And joyfully, the life I have chosen has landed me at a place of contentment. It gives me a feeling of accomplishment, not only for myself, but for others I've met along the way whom I've had the pleasure and the opportunity to influence in meaningful ways. And I can testify that I have been rewarded abundantly for staying on my path, in ways that far outweigh the trials and tribulation I met on the way to becoming uniquely me.

Unfortunately, even now, too many of us, lost to the institutional denial of our rights and privileges as American citizens are simply trying to survive. Not being able to look right or left, the fight to stay alive and out of prison, the struggle to rise above it all, they've had no opportunity to find their NorthStar much less to help others. I too, "but for the grace of God," could have been one of them but thanks to the influencers in my life and my community of Chickasaw Terrace, I stand tall and proud of who I am.

Life in Alabama, and pretty much everywhere in the South when I was born in the 1940s, was no panacea for Black people. In Mobile, the oldest port city in Alabama, the Jim Crow laws enacted immediately following the abolition of slavery were taken seriously. So serious in fact, that even after slavery was constitutionally abolished, the Clotilda, the last known slave ship to the Americas, under covert operation and on a $100,000 bet, transported 110 men, women, and children from Benin, West Africa landed in Alabama.

Thanks to Cudjoe Lewis, one of the slaves who came over on the Clotilda, our slave story has been recorded in the annals of Mobile history in Africa Town. Founded by Cudjoe in 1935, Africa Town holds and preserves the history of the descendants of the Clotilda slaves, one of whom you may know by name "Questlove" Ahmir Thompson, the multitalented musician. I am proud to say I became a tangential part of this history because I was at school with Cudjoe's niece five generations removed, Frankie Lewis Campbell who was a classmate and friend.

And even much later than that, Mobile was credited for the last lynching recorded of nineteen year-old Michael Donald on March 21, 1981! So, it should come as no surprise that when Blacks began to push back against the atrocities they faced, Alabama pushed harder. Alabama, which would later become the epicenter of the Civil Rights Movement, indeed has quite a history and a story to tell. Today, the Dora Franklin Finley African American Heritage Trail, founded by the late Dora Franklin Finley, provides a unique experience of the rich history of Mobile's African American culture highlighting our challenges, sucesses, and how we turned oppositions into opportunities after landing on the gulf shores of Alabama. Judge Karlos Finley, Dora's brother, serves as President, Board of Directors and cousin Eric Finley, today serves as the Director of Tours. All are friends of long standing.

Regardless of the social systems in place, (Jim Crow Laws) legally separating Blacks and whites, the South and all of the United States of America has been impacted by its indefatigable African Americans citizens, who from the days of slavery until now, have never given up their fight for freedom. As I observe some of the challenges of integration we face in these modern times, ironically and perhaps counter intuitively, segregation might have been an unwitting boon for members of my generation and those before me. Segregation, which forced most Blacks to live in humble surroundings far removed from the stately mansions of the wealthy white community you can still see in Mobile today, served as a buffer and created iron clad Black communities that protected and empowered their own. These humble cocoons where our culture could flourish and our values constantly reinforced, proved to be psychologically advantageous for us. Black folks, all over the South fighting the same struggles of oppression like my community, were extremely protective of its residents.

My world was nestled in Prichard, a suburb of Mobile, in a small, tight knit community known as Chickasaw Terrace. The community, in general, was not an economically thriving one, but it was infused with hope and love. Prichard was perhaps not really a suburb as we think of them today, because it was situated on the outskirts of Mobile where lower and middle class Blacks lived, and it was a diverse community. Our neighbors were a hardworking mix of people: day laborers, blue collar workers, and civil servants. We also had a few teachers, doctors, lawyers, and clergy. It was a community that staunchly took care of its own and fearlessly upheld the fight for Black freedom. This was the protective canopy of the world I grew up in.

Irrespective of one's station in life, domestic worker or principal, the church was the center of our community and held us together like glue. There were, of course, social circles and cliques but at the core of our community was love, protection, and the church. Church was an all-day thing on Sunday, so there was no 'not knowing' your neighbors. Everybody came together for fellowship, to worship and to pray for much needed uplifting to face another week in the white man's world.

More uncommon back then than in Black communities of today, I was the son of a single mother, Mabel Williams, and a father I hardly knew. With no ingrained memories of my dad, even before he died in an accident when I was a young boy, he played no role in my life or in defining who I would become. Not having a father was not something I dwelled on because there were many male role models in our community to look up to, and it was a nonissue, or so I thought. To be honest, I thought more about being fatherless as an adult than I did as a child—partly because I didn't know the difference. From the stereotypes African Americans inherited that imposed undue hardships, being a fatherless Black child raised in the 1940s the Jim Crow South, could have made me a statistic, a blip, another failure in America's social experiment. But I wasn't! Rather, inside of me burned a desire, a boundless wildfire, to be a change agent for my race, to claim my rightful place in this world, and to command a seat at any table. Bolstered by my community, I had faith that my life had meaning and purpose and I was loved, and there is nothing stronger or more nurturing than love. Love raised me up, gave me wings, and seeded my dreams. I was driven by purpose which eclipsed any angst I might have had around an absent father and despite the odds, I was poised to win.

Growing up in the South, both pre-and post-the Civil Rights era, made for interesting days. For Blacks in Alabama, it was a place of great cautionary tales. Like many states in the South, Alabama, used physical force, terror, economic intimidation, and psychological control to exert messages of low self-worth and negativity on its Black citizens. In any Black household there were constant debates, discussions, and warnings about how to keep safe from the Jim Crow Laws. Mothers would impose strict curfews on their children and lights might stay unlit longer to deter any rabble rouser.

As a youngster, I was surrounded by good people with great hearts who were all committed to my well-being, and this shielded me from the harsher realities of the environment in which I lived. My life seemed pretty good, despite the hostility. Notwithstanding its atrocious history, it was upon Alabama's shores that many tragedies and triumphs of the 50s and 60s played out. It was the state where many pioneering Black men and women said, 'no more!' Those words served to awaken the conscious minds of both Black and white citizens, mine included.

I vividly remembered two incidents that still impact my life today. The lynching and brutally beating of Emmett Till in 1955, in Mississippi and the death of my childhood friend (Johnny Wheat), who was run-over and left to die by a white man. I was 14 years old when Emmett Till died. I remember seeing his open casket, at the request of his mother, Mrs. Mamie Till-Bradley. Fearful and visually shaken, I thought I could be next in line. This is how we live during that time, in constant fear. But it was the faith and trust in God that got us through.

Unlike my father's side of the family, I was close with my mother's family. I knew very well who my mother was though she'd left for New York City when I was very young. The great migration was in full swing, and my mother's three sisters and her brother had already traveled north, seeking more than the South had to offer. That my mother would follow to make a good life—at least a better one—for herself and me was no surprise. She had fought hard to take me with her, but my grandmother insisted I was too young for the rough and tumble life of New York.

Back then, as droves of younger people left the South for the North to find prosperity, it was common that their offsprings were left behind in the care of relatives. I was raised in Grandma's household, and I was well cared for. I was separated, but never disconnected from my mother. Every week a letter would arrive, sometimes to my delight, with money. My grandmother had insisted that mother not lose touch with me and mother, it seems, had no intention of doing so. When she could, I'd get weekly phone calls, but best of all was when she'd visit. I can't say I didn't miss my mother or that it did not affect me, but as I said, I had a solid community, and it helped that many of my friends and classmates were being raised by their grandparents or other relatives. Because our culture believed in 'it takes a village,' it was an acceptable thing to do, and life went on uninterrupted.

My grandparents were loving. As an only child, they doted on me and in their home, I found stability and I thrived. In that loving, strict environment I never questioned why I was there but rather focused on the things I could control, which were always driven by being social and my academics. I was extremely focused on my academics and was a good student. I began developing into the precocious child I would become with my unique outlook on life and a firmness of mind.

Grandmother was stern and had a powerful presence. To me, she was a force of nature, yet she was loving and always kind. I never wanted for a hug or understanding when needed, or a good wallop if deserved. Those wallops, thank goodness, were few and far between. Ever desirous of not having a sore bottom, rest assured that I, who hated punishments, avoided doing anything that could cause a beating so I tended to be decently behaved. As a stay-at-home parent, grandma would make delicious food and be involved in my day-to-day life. That combination of being outgoing, disciplined and mentally fluent was my calling card to the world.

As important as my academics were, so was Sunday school. Every Sunday from morning till dusk was spent in church. I loved it when Sundays rolled around because it meant that I was able to interact with the other kids all day. It was a time of play, picnics, and general revelry for us children. Church became the rock upon which all our lives were built and a sanctuary to lay our burdens down and pray for a brighter future. Church too, became the place where the Civil Rights Movement went from a spark to a steady burning flame.

My grandfather, Will Todd, my first role model, was not as strict as grandma. I adored my grandfather, and he had an enormous impact on my life. Papa, as I called him, was very people-oriented and a most magnificent God-fearing man. Courageous, decisive, and dependable, he was a deacon in the church. Structure was his way and when I use the word puritanical to describe him and my grandmother, I am right on the money. That way of life worked well for them and shaped their expectations of me and for me. Because of Papa, I grew up wanting to make a difference. Through him I understood the importance of having a spiritual base, of giving, and of sharing our individual gifts with others. As one of the main go-to people in the community, Papa gave a lot, but never expected much in return. At times, people took advantage of him and he knew it, but he was never perturbed. Far more important to him was doing what he felt was right for others, especially those in need.

Papa worked hard to provide for his family and never missed a day of work at The International Paper Company. The company was about four miles from our home, which was a long distance away back then but seems like nothing today. Every day without fail he'd set off in the early morning to meet his responsibilities. After thirty-some years when he retired, he got a watch. I don't remember whether it was a gold watch or not, but he'd earned it for never missing a day of work. Unbelievable today.

Aside from being the key influencer in my life as well as a respected deacon in the church with his own designated seat in the front pew (and he'd remind anyone who forgot and sat in his seat), Papa became very involved in the civil rights issues of the times. Due to the intense feelings surrounding civil rights, Papa became very protective of us, just as other men in the community became of their families. With segregation and white supremacy being challenged, you could literally feel the volatility in the air at times and it weighed heavily on all of us. Those who were prepared to stand up, to push back against injustice were also well aware that they and their families could be targeted in some way, and that they might even lose their lives. Yet, that reality never deterred these brave men and women who knew that 'a change was gonna come,' from soldiering on.

My extended church family was one that I viewed respectfully. The deacons and men of the church all being role models to me were staunch believers in the Word. We took comfort and drew strength from worshiping at the altar of our God. A united force against all that threatened our well-being, these good people watched over us kids with hawk-like precision. That also came with the privilege to reprimand us verbally and physically if we got out of line.

Papa, like grandma, was a stickler for excellence and promoted it any way he could. One significant tradition I will always remember was when Papa would bring jars of candy to our school to hand out to students who were on good behavior and who were achieving their marks. That piece of candy meant a lot to us, because it affirmed the things that were so important in our lives, kindness, respect for community, social graces, and education. Papa did this a few times a year and he was always surrounded by eager students who'd tried their best all year to earn the coveted candy. So, if you talk about a significant moment in my life, this was one that was really key for me. I began taking on a lot of my grandfather's traits, doing the same things he'd done for others, but on a much larger scale when I became an adult.

When my grandmother died I was nine years old. It was a devastating loss for our family and a very, very sad day for me. I miss her to this day. My care fell to my aunts, but Papa was never far away. Papa, along with three of my aunts, Catherine Washington, who was a suitcase teacher in in Jackson, Alabama (meaning she commuted every week and came home on weekends), Aunt Maggie Singleton, and Aunt Alma Brown who'd moved back from New York, raised me in true "it takes a village" form. Aunt Maggie had two children: Helen Singleton Kirk (Cookie) and Angelo Singleton. Aunt Alma had one son Eric Williams (Penny). Aunt Catherine had no biological children but was a mother to us all. It was nice to have more family members around. I was close with my first cousins (Helen "Cookie", Penny, Angelo and with Kathy, the daughter of my uncle, Roy Todd, who lived in Norfolk, Virginia). We had limited contact back then, but we've stayed in touch over the years. Penny and Angelo are no longer with us, but I remain close with Cookie. These people were my family, and I was lucky to have them in my life.

After his retirement, Papa kept himself occupied by mowing lawns for the white folks across town and whenever possible, I would tag along. This was the first time I remember being in proximity to Anglo-Saxon whites. They were quite different from the Jewish people who ran most of the stores in our neighborhood. The Jewish merchants were kind. They were a blessing to our neighborhood because if anyone couldn't quite meet the expense of their groceries for the week, they would allow them to put it on credit. Although they didn't follow the Pope, I guessed, like me, they believed in the tenet of Pope Francis who said, "Rivers do not drink their own water; trees do not eat their own fruit, the sun does not shine on itself, and flowers do not spread their fragrance for others is a rule of nature. We are all born to help each other no matter how difficult it is. Life is good when you are happy; but much better when others are happy because of you." The help they offered our community made a difference in the quality of an already hard life. On the other hand, to the Anglo-Saxon folks in the big mansions, we were 'invisible.' The Jews too, were feeling the sting of racism and antisemitism despite the color of their skin as rampant racism was *de riguer.*

Even though races didn't mix, there were times when white folks would come to our neighborhood for no other reason than to shoot into known activists' homes as a warning for them to cease and desist their Civil Rights activities. These outright confrontations only made our community grow tighter and more determined. I got the benefit of not only protection from my community but a firsthand view of the brave, stalwart men and women who never backed down even in the face of danger. No matter who was saying what about our community or trying to quiet us down to avoid confrontation, my grandfather never wavered a single time in his conviction toward the march for freedom and his actions and his integrity were never questioned. I made sure too, that I was growing a courageous spine and the self-determination to be able to make a difference.

Fearlessness I recognized at an early age, was rooted in something other than we could readily see, hope. Thus, the importance of having a spiritual base. Giving and sharing "in spite of," came naturally for me as it was what I saw in my community. Realizing that there may be times when I was taken advantage of, like Papa I never allowed those disappointments to cast shade over the light of good deeds. Sure, I would be disappointed at times but I was never without hope.

Humility was drummed into us from the pulpit on Sundays, or by lessons taught at home during conversations at dinner. We knew of no other way to be. Have no doubt, I was mindful of the strict moral and religious standards I needed to observe. Humility was a given and rigorous discipline exacting yet welcomed by me. Spending Sundays at church learning about God, myself, and the moral way I wished to live my life helped me to remain humble. I also believe it shaped the life of service that would become my life's goal.

Still, I was a child and every now and again I would get into trouble, but never more than the occasional fight, or other minor teenage misdeeds like driving my aunt's car without permission. The one thing my friends could never get me to do, however, was skip class or engage in anything like stealing, for which one could go to jail. The things I did never amounted to anything so severe to be life changing. Only in Prichard could I have gained the maturity, wisdom, insight, non-negotiable determination, and the tools needed to address the challenges that were yet to come.

In New York, my mother had found work in the garment district. It was there that she met the gentleman who would become my stepfather, Roger Williams. A New York transplant from North Carolina, he worked with my mother. A U.S. Navy man, he loved my mother dearly. When they moved back to Mobile after I had graduated college we were in constant contact and as such spent a lot of family time together. Mr. Williams was a kind and gentle man, and he became an integral part of our family. I somehow preferred to call him Mr. Rogers. He taught me how to become a handyman, showing me how to repair cars and the like. It wasn't until much later when my children started calling him grandpa that I too began to call him grandpa. Mr. Rogers fully accepted me as his son and our family fully accepted him as family.

But like with many other families, there were family secrets. The things that were never discussed. The stories never told. Legendary Black family secrets. So, I was in elementary school when I learned I had a half-sister, Lois Riley, who lived with her father's family in Alabama. I didn't know much about the dynamics of that story, but she was my mother's daughter. I'm not sure if it was meant to be a secret as much as it just never came up or one of the pieces of information only divulged on a need to know basis, but somehow I learned about this around the time I did. One thing was for sure, she was not my stepfather's daughter as her birth had happened before my mother met her new husband. It was not a shock to me, and as with all things, I took the news of my sister in stride and embraced her like family. Though Lois and I were not close in the way of siblings growing up together, we remain in touch to this day acknowledging each other on special occasions with great affection. I am also in touch with Uncle Roy's daughter, Royce Catherine Todd, who now lives in Charlotte, North Carolina, as I am with Cookie.

With all the things that had taken place in my life, all I had seen, heard and experienced and the things yet to come, I have always known that following in my Papa's footsteps would allow me to take on anything and succeed. Prichard, where family, school, and the church played a pivotal role in shaping my life will always remain part of my story because it made me who I am.

TEACHABLE MOMENTS

The stories that are a part of us can be filled with a variety of emotions. They can be tragic, humble, encouraging, and sometimes without direction. As we grow into our best unique selves and prepare to serve the world, we must be mindful of this and draw on the strengths we have received, whether they are from adverse experiences or amazing opportunities. There is always something to be learned.

Take some time to think about how you have handled the situations in your life. If you're still school age, what things have lifted you up or those that are holding you back? How should you respond and

11

control unfavorable situations, rejecting that which doesn't serve you or others well? How can you find your voice and commit to your best journey possible? A life of crime, single parenthood, or not aspiring to be your best are intentional impediments to derail your progress. And, remember, it's not your career that matters most, but your morals and code of ethics. When those are aligned, you are aligned to help others. That is something that feels wonderful and cannot be replicated by anything else.

If you are starting or well into your career, ask yourself, what tough lessons did you learn? What things do you now know to avoid? How can your success become someone else's inspiration? How can you bring other people into your successful experience? Use your experiences to effect change, and never stop learning how to be an even more effective change agent. But to be fully accountable to yourself and to your community, you must understand that every action you take matters to everyone.

CHAPTER TWO

INVESTING IN PEOPLE

A stable life can be a pleasant life, yet it is not enough if there is not recognition of your circumstances or a desire to make life better for someone else too.

—Unknown

As a child, I didn't know exactly what a world stage was, but I knew it was bigger than Chickasaw Terrace. I wanted my life to play out on a larger stage than my little community and I knew there was more out there somewhere that would allow me to be of service in a way that crossed lines and boundaries. As an observant child, I spent a lot of time watching the people around me. It seemed to me that everyone, regardless of gender, creed, or politics, wanted similar things. The Jewish shopkeepers, the white employers, or the Black mothers, all sought a life of purpose, fulfillment, and joy. Yet there was this artificial barrier dividing people called race! I began to envision the role that I could play in making the world a better place, not just for me, but for every American citizen. To me that meant I should find a way to build bridges of unity to overcome the artificial barriers of race and culture.

Being a difference maker to one's immediate family and community is a great blessing and from a young age, this has always been the driving force, speaking to both my heart and mind. Intuitively, and before I fully realized the power of influence and the obligation its presence would hold in my life, my soul yearned to express this need for cross-cultural connections. To be an instrument of change was something I knew I'd somehow inherited and had to fulfill. So, there was never a single moment growing up where I doubted I'd have the opportunity to be who and what I wanted to become. Raised with the fortitude and conviction of people whose strong values, big dreams, and fearless demeanor was certain, I was seeded in that confidence. If I wanted it, it was as good as done. That was the message I internalized as a child and because of this, I was eager to pave my own path and define life on my terms. Even in the early years, I was not just a precocious child who longed for something great, I was a believer who had a faith that could move mountains.

There were times when that blustering confidence faltered a bit. Physically and materially, my life never lacked the basics. I had love, shelter, food, spiritual nourishment, and social engagements. Having all these things, however, should not be confused with feelings of completeness. I was always aware of an undertone of incompleteness—always aware that a certain kind of love was missing from my life. I believe this was a natural response to the absence of a mother and father directly raising me. That reality influenced me more than I had initially imagined, but it never overshadowed, crippled, or defined my life. Thankfully and gratefully, the gaps my parents lack of presence left in me were fulfilled by the fire within and the incredible mentorship I received. Because of my mentors, I would soon come to understand that a soul can be set on fire by anyone, who not only believes in you, but who also made the time to hold space for you and are committed to helping you find the tools needed to soar.

The more I learned about myself and the world around me, the more I wanted to be a part of the larger world beyond Chickasaw Terrace and that meant nurturing good relationships. I've had circles of friends and relationships with different groups since my early childhood, always seeking ways to maintain them. I have been deliberate, loyal, and strategic in my relationships and this shows because many have lasted a lifetime.

Education Paves the Path to Your Best Self

Even if we come into the world with a divine purpose, to realize its full potential, it has to be nurtured. As an adult, I now fully appreciate how my grandparents, and the people of Chickasaw Terrace nurtured the uniquely designed person I was for that place—and in that time. As I would find out, and not coincidentally, when you find and fully live in your passion, success has already found you. The challenge is, will you recognize it?

Others would often look at me and label me intelligent, gifted, talented and articulate. I did skip a grade in elementary school and graduated high school by the time I was sixteen, so, yes, I guess maybe I was gifted and was in a hurry to move toward my bliss. At intersecting points in life, a choice needs to be made on which path to follow. For me, my path was always education. Choosing education was one of the easiest decisions I'd ever had to make. The insistence of everyone around me that I become a well-educated man mirrored my craving for all the opportunities that education could provide. Why education? Because all the people who were thriving and moving in the circles I desired to be in, were educated. They always seem to have more access to the finer homes, cars, clothes, and the most prestigious social clubs.

Early Years

I attended a school just down the street from our home called New Chickasaw Terrace Elementary and was there until I completed eighth grade. School became something I laser focused on and it was an amazing experience. It was the start of making lifelong friends, such as my adopted sisters, Doris, and Stella Boykins, and Rollie Steele who was with me all the way through high school and that has been most rewarding. Stella is now deceased, but Doris and I have maintained our relationship all these years and have shared beautiful memories. Also included in this list are Clara Pogue and her brother Johnny Pogue, Johnny Scruggs, Elisha "Tony" Powe, Jesse James Dueberry, Freddie Cooley, George Archibald Stephens, who became my brother-in-law, and Juliette Summerville (now Smith). My friendship with Juliette began in ninth grade and continued through college.

I tend to be a practical person, more given over to logic than emotions. Like Papa, I never missed a day of school making it all the way through with a perfect attendance record. I even went to school on the day my grandmother passed away. People were shocked but I knew that there was nothing I could do at home and I also knew it was what grandma would have wanted. In my mind, the greatest way to honor her and acknowledge her love and the sacrifices she made for me would be to carry on by passing the batons of striving and hope she'd instilled in me to the next generation.

School offered me peace and solace on days when neither were present. When kids in the neighborhood would taunt me about being different, there were others just like me who were excited to learn and were ready to blaze trails. We all came from the same neighborhood, but some people had different aspirations. I wanted to be with the group who dreamed of a different future than the options that existed in Chickasaw Terrace. The unspoken—perhaps even unintended—saving grace for me was that I now had friends at school to bridge the gaps of loneliness at home. As I sought out healthy friendships, I also became a relationship connector. Whether it was for dating, events, friendships, or church, it made me feel useful. One such was for my elementary school childhood friend, Johnny Lee Wheat, who wanted to meet these two girls he fancied, dreaming they'd become his girlfriends. I made a successful introduction and felt very special because this made Johnny happy. None of us were to know what would happen next and to our distress and sorrow, Johnny was killed in a hit and run car accident while we were in High School.

Making social connections was important to me from the youngest age and still is to me to this very day. Being a connector is something I enjoyed immensely and is a skill that runs strong in me even now. It is the foundation upon which I've built my life of purpose and these connections have afforded me opportunities throughout this world I could never have imagined in Chickasaw Terrace. It isn't always easy and sometimes it is very hard work, but it is a calling and I am dedicated to its undertaking.

The Power of Social Impact

Being people-oriented and sociable, my mind was ever-present to my surroundings, and I was keen to seek out like-minded individuals. With them, I felt I belonged, I felt accepted, and so I found myself in an environment well-suited to my personality; and it brought me much joy. Social people are often good at the art of persuasion and communication. At school, I'd learned about rhetoric, and about how to speak in a manner that made others take note of what I had to say. One of the earliest uses of my rhetorical skills came when I was in eighth grade and was invited to participate in the school's oratorical contest. There was a certain pride and dignity in the school having various contests to demonstrate their students' outstanding qualities and talents. That day, I recited the Lord's Prayer. This contest was significant to me, not because I wanted to hear myself talk, but because I wanted to demonstrate that I could have something to say that my peers might want to hear. The captivated audience, who'd probably heard the Lord's Prayer said a thousand times, garnered me with a loud ovation and I ended up the winner of the contest. By all accounts, this became the beginning of me using my voice to communicate my hopes, wishes, and desires to others.

Teachers and selected members of our community were the judges of many of these competitions, and students considered them a big deal. Community competitions were fun also. Everyone would gather to decorate the MayPole on May Day and there were other opportunities to showcase our skills and appreciation for arts and culture. These were all important ways to strengthen our community's ties. We needed each other and events like these helped us find joy despite the oppression. By the time I left elementary school, I was a confident and emboldened lad, and already had a strong idea of my path and trajectory.

When it was time for high school, I attended Mobile County Training School, known as MCTS. Like elementary school, this was the local Black kid's high school in the area, but the student body came from a wider area than just Chickasaw Terrace. Transitioning to high school was a different experience from anything I had ever encountered in my life. Suddenly, I was in an unfamiliar environment with people I really did not know, though we were all Black, we represented the caste system that was firmly in place.

Doubt

Despite the love and stability, I had in my life growing up, as noted I couldn't completely escape being scarred by absent parents. For years, I was unable to articulate or acknowledge that there was a missing part of me. But there would be times when feelings of self-doubt or abandonment would seek to halt my trajectory. That was when I knew I had to pause, look inside, and deal with these issues head-on. If I did not know it then, I know it to be true today that parental love is important for that feeling of total acceptance. I knew I was rooted in the unconditional love but the absence of my parents still left a kernel of something missing. Sometimes my mind wrestled with my perceived abandonment, and my soul surely grappled with unrecognized pain. In those moments, the wheels might have come off. I was lucky to have my community to turn to when I needed someone to rely on, but no one can ever replace parents. For me, the men in the church and community, as well as my Papa were my bedrock and role models. They were pivotal in demonstrating how I could grow into a responsible, compassionate, and God-fearing man. I accepted my situation as something that further defined my uniqueness. And with my faith firmly placed in my creator, I came face-to-face with the man who I was and the man I wanted to become. I chose my call to serve over self-pity.

It was at this point that I first had to reckon my bouts of self-doubt. Having people from different backgrounds and perspectives made me realize that if I was going to survive, I had to overcome any adversity and set my sights on becoming a leader. It was then that I came to understand that my feeling of self-doubt stemmed from my perceived abandonment by my parents and from facing this new caste system that was never an issue in Chickasaw. The new burden of having to contend with my God-given skin color, which would have failed the paper bag test, was disconcerting. I began to appreciate my ability to be introspective. Addressing these doubts meant that I first needed to find "me" in all my iterations because, in order to grow and move toward realizing my dream, I first had to remove hindering thoughts. To scale barriers, and really get in there and become involved—really fight for what I wanted—I had to solidify my values. What I wanted was to achieve a higher quality of life and being in leadership was critical to making that happen. In high school, this meant joining the social clubs and getting involved irrespective of my fears.

Similar to my experience in elementary school, in High School, the time came when I had to leave some of my friends behind in order to create a new group of people with whom I was more aligned. This was not done in a callous way or with a light heart. It wasn't that I felt I was better. It was more that I'd never be the man I was designed to be if I didn't allow unhealthy friendships to fall away. I knew with certainty that after high school I was going to college, and my aim was to go as far up the education ladder as I could. Making this choice to me meant leading from in-front. But whether leading from in front or from behind, acute choices have to be made along our journey...ones that are right just for you.

Quite a few of my elementary school friends did not transition to Mobile County Training School (MCTS) for one reason or the other, or in situations I knew I wanted to stay clear of. I didn't feel great about leaving them behind, but these are the crossroads where choices have to be made and the wrong choice could alter one's life in drastic ways. So, my social circle was diminished, and I needed to expand it. I was eager to make high school an experience that would continue to help me with all my future aspirations. To achieve my plan, I grew serious about defining my limits and where I could become limitless. I naturally flowed with those who had their own desires and ambitions, and it is with fondness that I call many of these people friends to this day. But first I had to be accepted. Each of us had our own goals, some grand and some just enough to get by.

There was no shortage of social clubs at MTCS but many were difficult to get into. One of those clubs was Mrs. Valena Withers McCants'

"The Artisan's Club," and it was the top club. Its members were students like me—with lofty ambitions. I wanted to be surrounded by their energy and vision because I felt that they complemented mine, I had to work very hard to get an invitation. Since the people in the clubs really didn't know me, it fell upon my shoulders to become known and to show them that I had what it took to be a club member. All I knew was that I needed to be included in this prestigious club! With the students doing the inviting, and then voting on who could join, I had to reach out to them and let them know—without a doubt—that I was interested and that choosing me would prove to be an asset for their club.

In the process of lobbying for invitations, I learned a few important things. First, I learned not to be shy about asking for the things that I wanted. Second, I had to set myself to a higher personal standard than many others because of the privilege inherent in their pedigree. Thirdly, I began to comprehend the extent to which meaningful social circles were essential because I saw how much friends mattered. I somehow was able to meet all three criteria necessary to reach my goal of inclusion in several prestigious clubs.

The exposure and experience I gained by being in those clubs helped me to become more confident. I was able to hone my social skills yet remain authentic. Mindful of my purpose and aspirations I doubled down on every effort to make meaningful contributions to the clubs. Thank goodness for the selection process because it prepared me for my climb. Had I just shown up and said, "Hey, here I am, let me join," I would not have learned all that I needed to navigate the life I had chosen for myself.

The high school band was also very prestigious, and I needed to be a member of that band too. The band's high flying members' reputation dovetailed with who I wanted to become. I used my newly honed power of influence getting into The Artisan Club to get into the band. My life would have been easier had I played sports as the sports guys became automatic stars. I was not a sports guy. Never have been. And to be honest that route didn't pique my interests one bit, nor would it have allowed me to demonstrate my best skills. Joining the band offered me the best of both worlds. I got to travel to football games and other activities where the band played. I also participated in parades and all types of events. In the band I was well immersed in the school spirit, and felt a sense of belonging, especially because I was part of something that mattered to me.

But the group I wanted—really wanted to connect with, were the superstars. They didn't belong to a club. They were simply a group that consisted of high achieving individuals who had intentionally come together to develop a long standing friendship. Unlike people who randomly connected and formed bonds, this group was deliberate and focused. There were a lot of cliques and clubs at MCTS but there was nothing quite like this exclusive group of 'friends.' One couldn't even apply to be a part of this group. You had to be recommended by an already existing member. The signature social achievement of my high school experience was being invited into the group. Billy Samuel was the group member who connected me to this group of eight. I became number 9. Billy was from a neighboring community, and we had a lot in common in terms of our family dynamics. After taking note of my personality and seeing it as a complimentary fit for this group of friends, he recommended me, and I was accepted.

An instant energy and excitement overtook me. I was now a part of a group of people who were high achievers, and who refused to allow prejudices and other negativities to hold them back. The group members were Billy Warren Samuels, William Anderson Crenshaw, George Lovejoy, Rayford Howard Campbell, LeRoy Hamilton, John Adams, Peggy Ann Scott, Juliette Summerville, and me. That I could be my authentic self with these people was a gift that kept on giving. It was an unforgettable experience. Through all the groups I was a part of, I learned lessons and sharpened skills. The Big 9 stuck close to each other like super glue. Energized by our visions and aspirations, we were the envy of many of our classmates. There was a natural prejudice that existed toward us at school and those who were not a part of our group could be spiteful—sometimes to the point of accusing us of trying to act like a "whitie." We were told we would

21

never fit into the white world, no matter how hard we tried. Without each other, those words could have been painful. But as a strong group we let the insults roll right off our backs. Undeterred, we took on the types of responsibilities and activities at school and at home that would elevate us to be leaders of change. Eventually, when a need arose that had to be attended to, people would look to us. Out of the nine of us in this group, one headed up the student newspaper, several were athletes, there was a beauty contest winner, and a number of us were in the band, including me. What was for sure, we were all natural born leaders. Our message was clear so when a need arose that had to be attended to, people would look to us to represent our school externally and competitively. We shared our experiences with our extended friends (Doris Boykins, Constance Portis, Rollie Steele, Delia Retic, etc.) They too were leaders.

The Big 9 cultivated relationships off campus, and with students from our rival school who also had big goals and were similarly laser focused on how they wanted their future to unfold. Despite my desire to be a self-driving force of my future, I knew there was strength in numbers and as a group we grew more energized. It is quite ironic that some of my high school rivalries became my best friends. Vincent Henderson, who attended Central High School and is a highly successful culinary expert. The Reverend LeBaron Taylor attended Most Pure Heart of Mary Catholic School is an Episcopal Priest and Donald Buck, Most Pure Heart of Mary High School , an Executive with IBM. Although Vincent and Donald are no longer with us, LeBaron is still a good friend today. A group of young ladies at our rivalry school, Central High, who shared the same values and were leaders in their own rights are very close friends today as well. They are Janice Harris (Brazier), Andreda Wilkins (Pruitt), Thelma Battle (Thrash), Ardenia Wilkins (Johnson) and Esther Nettles (Rauch).

As exhilarating as the experience was, at times it was overwhelming. I needed a firm guiding hand from a seasoned mentor, perhaps someone who had already navigated the path to this world of opportunity. One person who changed my life and helped prepare me for who

I was to become was Dr. Gaines Thompson. Many members from the Big 9 went on to have successful careers and lives, including me.

Dr. Gaines Thompson was a successful dentist from a neighboring upscale Black community. From a prominent family, his father was a physician, and his mother, the first African American pharmacist in the state of Alabama. Dr. Thompson was well-schooled in the social graces, and his abilities to effectively guide and mold me for the world I desired to enter made him an even more desirable mentor for me. Assimilating for people not considered "American" was a path to upward mobility. For me it meant I had a chance to be in the rooms where it happens and therefore opened the door for cultural bridge building. When I met Dr. Thompson, he was a part of the prestigious Striker's Club, which was a social organization for Blacks. They were well known by everyone in Mobile and were actively involved in major events including Mardi Gras, which incidentally started in Mobile before it became the cultural mainstay in New Orleans. It is still a vibrant event today in Mobile.

Dr. Thompson took me under his wing and taught me everything I needed to know in order to succeed in the life I aspired to have and he informed me just what that life would require of me. From basics such as the proper use of a knife and fork, where and when to place my napkin during a meal, how to wear Black Tie, and how to dress for different occasions. He showed me the importance of verbal intonations and nonverbal communication. As my advisor, he helped me become more fluent in navigating important topics such as politics, career choices, social opportunities; and he taught me basic survival skills in order to navigate the white culture. To me, this training was every bit as important as my academics. It helped me gain unshakable confidence in social settings where I may have otherwise been less polished. The things I learned from Dr. Thompson enriched my life a level above my experiences up to that point.

Joining Dr. Thompson's societal groups gave me access to a new social circle in Mobile—one which enlightened me and prepared me for the wider world beyond Chickasaw. Literally, he made me a part of his family, investing in my success the way a father might have a son. And here I stand today in a place where I think he would have been very proud.

Everyone from the South knows what a big deal a debutante ball is to a young woman and her parents. Dr. Gaines Thompson, and Mrs. Valena Withers McCants, chaired the Debutante Cotillion event and it was no coincidence that they chose me when I was a sophomore in college as a debutante escort. Sponsored by the Striker's Club, The Debutante Cotillion was, and still is, a way to introduce male children to female Debutantes of similar status to establish lifelong connections. I gladly agreed. It was an opportunity to prove myself to the families that were part of high society. As a chosen escort, I had the opportunity to meet influential people while helping to introduce these well-rounded young women into society.

Mrs. Valena Withers McCants was another person who had a tremendous influence on my life. As my ninth-grade teacher, she was a revered and well-respected woman in the community, who spearheaded many activities in the neighborhood. Her life underscored for me the reason I needed to step out into the world to do my very best in helping to transform it into a more equitable place for those who lived in Chickasaw. Mrs. Valena Wither McCants became a sounding board for my "next moves and ideas," and helped me perfect the skills needed to deliver on that vision.

A visionary herself, she and Dr. Gaines Thompson framed and bookended this period of my life and were a part of all the significant events happening during my time in high school. She is still alive and now in her late nineties. Undoubtedly a well-lived life, she is still very much a woman who has a heart for caring and a mind for action. She demonstrated with her life, one of her favorite sayings, "To whom much is given, much is expected." I was given a lot, and that meant I had a debt to pay to mankind. In return for my life's grace, I needed to venture out and focus on making people's lives better in some way.

The Strikers, founded in 1933, was an all-male group that consisted of professionals and like-minded people of a certain social class who had a societal authority that could not be ignored. Dr. Gaines

Thompson was a Striker and becoming a part of the Strikers mattered greatly to me. The Strikers Club quite literally helped the people it mentored strike on opportunities to elevate their social status and gain access into the white community to better understand how to elevate our own communities. They were the first group to integrate the hotels and the restaurants in Mobile as they were able to break down the caste system a bit, opening doors for many people. In time, I became the youngest member in that organization of very prominent Black men and I am proud of the work I did that helped the Strikers in their efforts to make a major impact in the Mobile community. With that success under my belt, I had now accomplished a long sought after goal, and that win motivated me to keep moving the goal post further and further out toward equality. It was through the Strikers Club that I developed a personal relationship with the late Philip Tyus, Joseph McCray, Walter "Pep' Rice, and David Thomas Sr. Though no longer with us, I have great memories of their friendship today.

By sharing these things, I am categorically not intimating in the least, Black inferiority or making a class judgment nor am I advocating assimilation of white standards. As an observer of human nature, I knew what it took to get to the point where logic could be heard. All the moves I made were strategic. If I wanted to be a change agent, change required both strategic and tactical planning. One must use the tools in their hands to chisel away at any notion of Black inferiority and gaining access into white society was the first strike of my chisel to clearly show that as Black people we were no different from anyone else and, in fact, could stand on par with any man on any ground. But it is hard to make a plan of action if one does not know the rules of engagement.

What all this simply means is, when you have focus, a direction, a goal, and understand the rules of the game, your impact, and the results you achieve can be profound. It can be hard to know what to do if you don't know what others have done before you. That's why it is so important to understand Black history. Like Frederick Douglas, Harriet Tubman, and like so many other freedom fighters for the Black community.

Like Dr. Thompson and Mrs. McCants, many others poured faith into my half-empty glass. I am not a self-made man, but a man who has been elevated by those who believed in me. To those who invested their time into my growth, I was glad to accept it as a gift, and committed that I would not and did not squander it. Even on the occasion when I would feel lazy, tired, or disappointed, like any kid on a sprint to purpose, I assuage my guilt and allowed myself some grace, knowing that the day would pass, and I would be back on track. I learned it was important to take a moment and breathe.

Finding Meaning Sometimes Means Making Choices

Lessons can be painful but necessary. They are met at every crossroad in life and they focus on our choices. The right choice can make a positive difference, and the wrong choice can spiral us into an abyss. I've often heard it said that the top five people in your immediate circle define your orbit and trajectory. Perhaps that is why I made the conscious choice to surround myself with strivers.

Education to me was the golden key to recognition, access, and a level of power and influence to make life better for those I had to leave behind. Some people may never understand why you make certain choices, but you must trust your instincts and put your faith into practice. The results will usually speak for themselves.

It Always Comes Back to the Spiritual Foundation: For Every Disappointment You Receive You Can Always Gain Perspective Through Your Faith in God.

I am a survivor because of love and guidance. Their presence in my life helped me avoid some of the psychological conditioning of racism. With a deceased father, and an absent mother, I would have been a prime candidate for significant psychological damage. But the people who loved and cared for me pushed me to become a better person despite life's strikes. My spiritual foundation was the rock upon which I built my house. Faith, trust, and humility are the walls of that house.

I couldn't have landed in a better place to grow up. I see God's plan in everything I do, and it was right for me to have traveled this particular path of spiritual development to spiritual maturity. High school was a defining period on my life path. It helped me better understand who I was and how to claim my power. If I were going to make a difference in this world, the choices I made would have to be grounded in my spiritual foundation, and without question they were. I truly believe that when we say yes to God unbounded opportunities find us.

Developing My Best High School and College Experiences

I wasn't blind or stupid. To the contrary. It was the mid-nineteen fifties, and I was well aware of the limited career opportunities I had at that point. There would be no open doors or opportunities for me in becoming a corporate CEO. My best chance was to become a doctor, lawyer, or teacher if I wanted to earn status as a member of "high society—which meant financial sustainability and opportunities." Normal and respectable occupations for Blacks back then were to become a postal worker, a fireman, or to take on service jobs of that ilk. My heart and personality knew those 'normal' jobs were not for me. I also knew that if I were to become a doctor or lawyer I would be limited to treating and representing only those in our Black communities. Let me explain this. At first, being a medical doctor was the path that I thought would be ideal for me. In time, I realized that there were all sorts of doctors, and a doctorate in education would be a more suitable way for me to expand my sphere of influence to a much broader audience. This was empowering for a young guy from Prichard. Hence my decision to pursue education to as far as my abilities allowed. All these massive goals— financial, community-oriented, and spiritual—were ones I was glad to work toward, and I gave it my all.

I am not inclined to follow, but rather to lead. However, after high school I followed some friends to Tuskegee for college. It was a glaring mistake. I ended up there because Billy and another friend, John Adams, decided to attend Tuskegee College. Guess how long I lasted? Two weeks! Immediately recognizing my mistake, I faked an illness and high-tailed it home. From this debacle I'd learned another valuable lesson about being a follower. At home, I had to contend with the challenging question of, what now?

Tuskegee Institute, founded in 1881 as a teacher's college, was a well-known historically Black school. It boasted Booker T. Washington as its first principal and graduated many outstanding alumni including Claude McKay, Ralph Ellison, MLK's attorney Chauncey Eskridge, Lionel Ritchie and The Commodores and Tom Joyner. Considered a first class institution for educating Black teachers, it was led by esteemed professors such as George Washington Carver and four star general Tuskegee Airman General Daniel "Chappe" James. The college was as prestigious as any and its reputation was indeed stellar. But it was not the right place for me.

Another lesson I learned was that making mistakes doesn't have to be the end of the world. When I recognized that I'd made the wrong choice, I acted without hesitation. This was my opportunity to change what didn't work out and get on the right path, rather than to dwell on the negative or suffer in silence. Leaving the Artisan Club and going to Tuskegee were two defining moments in my life where I had taken the wrong path and given a chance to correct them, thankfully, getting the ship back on course. Choice is something that will always resonate with me.

My next move was to find a place where I could thrive. Alabama State College, later known as Alabama State University, was where I ended up. Back in high school, every day I would get on the bus and head to school, going past the high school for white kids. I would observe what I saw knowing that the time would come when change would be inevitable. I also knew that I was going to be a part of that change. What I was beginning to realize was that people were generally good folks doing the best they could with what they had. Everyone was on a learning curve, and in the face of danger and racial tension, it was natural for folks to try to protect their families at all costs. False perceptions of others meant that like-folks stuck together with what they knew. That was just the way it was done. I had always wanted to move beyond that, but I had no idea how to get there. I had to figure it out and observing people beyond their masks gave me insight on what I needed to do to break down these psychologically induced barriers in an attempt to build bridges to a brighter future.

My vision was way beyond just the moment, already looking over the horizon to the endless possibilities of a free world for Black folks.

TEACHABLE MOMENTS: ALWAYS LOOKING FOR A BETTER WAY

If I could offer a free gift to a young person, it would be that they realize the importance of their high school years and the opportunities it could provide if taken advantage of. By all measures, it is the gateway to adulthood. It is a time to create opportunities for success and a time to make lifelong friendships. In my youth, education was the key to a brighter future in the Black community and to making things happen, especially with limited resources. Education taught us about our inalienable rights, and education connected us to the majority of society. I realize that high school today is not what it used to be, and that our culture and society has drastically shifted from the 1950s and 1960s. High school now can be such a harsh and exclusive place for kids—especially if they are deemed as different. We experienced bullying, cliques, lack of government funds to support basic tools needed to operate a school—all of it; but certainly not to the scale that exists today in our Black communities. But for me it was indeed a place that was much better than the streets.

Another gift I would give to young people is the wisdom to be selective about the company they keep. Being around people who lift you up is an indication of the heights you might reach. This has been important to me my entire life and I cannot begin to tell you the difference it has made to my journey. I've had enormous opportunities to meet stellar men and women performing at the top of their game. Many of these relationships often turned into lifelong friendships. Billy Samuels, for example, is someone I still chat with every year on his birthday of December 26th. We talk for a long while, catch up on current events, and have some laughs about the past. This friendship remains valuable to me because it is a connection with an achiever who helped lift me up, and who played a part in setting the stage for me to achieve my dreams. These friendships are a yardstick to my past, so I can appreciate the distance I have traveled.

You can have a life well-lived if you choose to be of service to others. But it is important to remember that you must live with a purpose in order to have an impact on others' lives. This is my perspective, but my actions have proven to be effective. Mistakes are a part of growing and maturing. There were times when I followed friends and went along with the flow even when I knew it wasn't the right way for me. That was a part of my desire to be accepted and to belong. You may have followed the crowd too. But a point will come when you'll have to do what will give you your best chance for a successful outcome. This happened for me when I broke away from Mrs. Valena Withers McCants' club to join a new club with a new teacher. I look back at that in regret, and I will tell you that she understood the decision. It didn't change her fondness for me or willingness to help me on my journey. The mantra for the club was: Once an Artisan, always an Artisan. It proved to be true.

Never stop hoping for a better world. I find that hope is in short supply these days with the people who need it most—children— struggling to find their identities in this world. So many of them have been denied the structure for success that comes from a solid community and grounded spirituality.

Being here is a blessing that I cherish. Each day is valuable, and I understand that better because of how many friends and classmates are now gone. It weighs heavily on my heart at times and reminds me that life is about constant growth and renewal. There can be no contentment in resting on my laurels—not when these are such pressing times in our world. Sure, these challenges have always been there, sometimes intense, and other times lingering in the undertones of society but as God's word is "the word;" hope springs eternal.

When I hear about how I've impacted others' lives, I am reminded that I am still alive and able, and therefore I am called to continue to try to make a difference, to start a new dialogue about the wonderful "what ifs" of life.

When I reflect on the pivotal moments of my life, I realize that I didn't always understand them at the time. I was given opportunities that I grew into, and that I explored with great vigor and curiosity. Now they make sense, and I understand better the lessons learned. And so many of them circle back to being of service to others. I believe that when one door closes, it closes for a good reason, and if you are aware of your surroundings, another door will open. This does require an element of faith. If you are faithful, if you are a true believer, and if you have put your trust in God, you don't have to understand everything right away.

Things can have their season and unfold for you when the time is right. You can stop frustrating yourself with questions like: Why did this door close? Why did this happen here for me? Why did I lose this? Why did I experience tragedies...disappointments...frustrations?

There have been times when I was held back because of these questions. I get it now and I do see the brilliance of God in all that I've touched. It is as if he was saying, "Okay, fine, you are going down this path, but this is not the path that you should go down." Gaining this understanding has helped me to spiritual maturity.

The Church gave me the confidence, faith, trust, and courage to continue to hope, believe and trust in spite of those who felt it would be better if I just "gave it a rest." I have stood at the altar of doubt, and to overcome it I have had to lean on the love that comes from spirituality and from being surrounded by good people.

CHAPTER THREE

EASY DECISION

"The time is always right to do what is right."

—Dr. Martin Luther King, Jr.

My College Years

After the debacle at Tuskegee, I got accepted to Alabama State College's (ASC) two-year program (The Branch) in Mobile in 1957, at the age of seventeen. As a branch of the main campus in Montgomery, I would spend the next two years completing my coursework before transferring to the main campus. It was here that I met Dr. Sanford Bishop, Head and Dean of the school, who also had a major influence on my life. He was a strong and caring leader who had high standards of achievement for students. He took a personal interest in us both off and on campus. I vividly recall that he would call our parents or family members if we were operating out of line. If we were absent from school for a period of time, he visited our homes to see why. He required us to attend weekly chapel appropriately dressed (shirt and tie) and to actively participate in campus activities.

My move from ASC's Mobile campus to the Montgomery campus to complete my college degree in 1959, came on the heels of some of the greatest and most inspirational activists of the Civil Rights movement. Just four years previous, in 1955, Rosa Parks had refused to give up her seat on the bus to a white passenger. This led to the year-long

Montgomery bus boycott, considered the first fundamental disobedience event in the Civil Rights protest against segregation laws. It also served to galvanize the NAACP that ramped up its activities against racism. The energy around campus at the time I arrived was palpable and kinetic as talks of integration bubbled up for attention. Though the protests had not yet taken full foothold toward massive change, it was obvious to me that change was on the way.

Change demanded stamina and non-negotiable will. Thankfully, I had more than my fair share and I didn't give up. Had I allowed myself to be crushed under the weight of racism, I would have missed out on what turned out to be a robust time with myriad opportunities to positively impact change for the Black community. For the kinds of dreams I held, the fiery times and the great Civil Rights leaders who emerged during this time were empowering. Their mission dove-tailed with my own.

Still, I was in such a new world in Montgomery. It was my first time away from home (because I didn't count my two-week experiment at Tuskegee), and for me, it began a new cycle of consciousness. In Montgomery, the Civil Rights Movement was in full swing, and I was ready to be a part of the fray. Taking up the mantle for civil justice was the charismatic Baptist minister, Martin Luther King, Jr. who became one of the most prominent leaders of the Civil Rights Movement. Montgomery, being an epicenter of the movement, was going through serious reverberations from the political and social Civil Rights activities taking place. Helmed by a super racist governor at that time, John Patterson, who vehemently discouraged the disbanding of Jim Crow Laws as did many whites. With his mantra of "segregation now, segregation tomorrow, segregation forever" his rhetoric encouraged many disgruntled whites to try to enforce the status quo of fear. This gave rise to stealth operations by white groups. The surge of the KKK, a group that was founded in 1865 that acted with impunity to protect white supremacy, was a direct result of people like Patterson. Whites, in an attempt to enforce the status quo, upped their violent activities against Blacks. Yet, nothing could dampen their sense of hopefulness, and no one could relay that optimism better than Dr. Martin Luther King, Jr. Inspiring change through action and peaceful protest, even in the face of barbaric attacks from the other side, earned King the respect of many political heavyweights. Nothing could move him off his point of peaceful protest. In fact, just the opposite. His tenacity would eventually cost him his life when he was gunned down in the state of Tennessee in 1968.

It was a tense and exciting time to start at the college and I was ripe in personality and passion to become a part of this mission of liberty for all. Yes, all of this appealed to me greatly and I became quite involved. I had a purpose to fulfill in this pursuit, as well. I didn't just want to receive the benefits of the cause, I wanted to be of service to it. This led to many uncomfortable situations while participating in activism. I had to exercise safety and caution.

Planting My Seeds of Civil Discourse

The college was within walking distance of the governor's office. Diagonally across from the capital was the Dexter Avenue Baptist Church where Dr. Martin Luther King, Jr. the up and coming young, inspirational minister presided. Between his church and campus was another church, that of MLK's friend Ralph Abernathy. With their fiery and impassioned oratory against Jim Crow Laws, it wasn't any wonder Montgomery and several southern cities had students' uprisings at many historically Black colleges.

I made the most of my opportunities in Montgomery and joined the newspaper staff. It was a wonderful place to be. I did a regular column, *Spotlights on Campus*, where I interviewed four students and highlighted them for outstanding accomplishments. This was what I was known for. As I created these features I began developing relationships with people engaged in the mainstream of things beyond campus. This gave me the chance to be in the mix of everything on campus and sometimes beyond. For me, placing a spotlight on these people through feature articles opened up a world of possibilities in my mind. I also began to appreciate that our community had a plethora of untapped resources that could positively change the world. With change happening all around me, it was natural that I would want to be a part of it all.

I began attending civil rights rallies on and off campus. At many of these rallies MLK, Abernathy, and other notable activists were in attendance. It's also important to note that we were a state supported school, run by the governor—who was not in alignment with Black liberation, so going to these rallies was risky. There were so many rules around what we could and could not do as students that one never felt safe. Eventually, the school was ordered to be locked down and if anyone stepped off campus they could be arrested and sent to jail. Going to jail wasn't uncommon and oftentimes not provoked.

I was cautious because the dorm where I lived was vulnerable. Most of the dorms on campus were central to the campus, but not mine. Referred to as the barracks, my dorm was on the edge of the campus which made it easy for those who wished to attack, harm, or even bomb our residences and places of worship to carry out their actions in secret. It was a constant worry for students in the barracks and it was an upsetting and fearful time—always. No one should have to live with the uncertainty that at any given time they could be attacked. Not everyone survived the day-to-day hassle. Many opted to leave school or transfer out. For me, this daily duress came with a renewed determination to become a difference maker.

Spreading a Hopeful Message Soothing the Panicked Heart

Out of all the rallies and peaceful protests I attended, one stands out in particular. This meeting was being held at Ralph Abernathy's church. The place was standing room only from the many in attendance. I will always remember Dr. Martin Luther King Jr. standing up, and in his calm, warm but authoritative voice, telling us we were surrounded by policemen on horseback and on foot, and that we should remain very calm and not panic. I immediately felt a sense of dread from the congregation gathered which added to my jitters. It wasn't easy to trust the police and I was not feeling calm. Who would, in such a situation? Nobody could say for certain what would happen. We could only hope and pray that they would do what they were meant to do—keep the peace.

That day became another defining moment for me, a particularly challenging one too. At that time there were frequent bombings of homes and businesses and people were losing their lives. Being shot at just for demonstration was *de rigueur* and honestly, I wasn't sure whether the church was going to be bombed or not. It sounds frightening because it was. I did the only thing I knew how to do, I started praying. Everyone joined in prayer and soon it was time to leave the church and make our way back to the campus. Our brave and committed leaders said they would lead us out of the church, and someone would escort us back to campus. Thank goodness, because this was not the age of cell phones where you could call someone for help if you were in danger.

Standing up for what is just when I was not sure I was going to survive was one of the most frightening things I ever experienced. It takes a level of faith and utter commitment to a cause to make such a decision, however, once you engage with the determination for change it becomes a fire in your soul and something you're willing to risk your life for. It becomes a statement of 'it's better to die on my feet than crawl on my knees,' and it becomes the sacrifice one is willing to make for their freedom and that of their progeny. It is a selfless and patriotic sacrifice—one that puts the needs of the many before the individual needs of the one. That night it was a long walk back to the campus, despite it not being a long distance. The march had been on constant replay on the news, and it was quite intense for everyone. So, immediately after returning to campus, I called my mother, Papa, and other family members to let them know I was okay. They breathed such a collective sigh of relief.

Many Black students chose to return home from college because they did not want their families to be targets of violence. This was particularly true of students from rural areas, farming areas, and those whose parents still worked for white families and white businesses. These white folks would tell parents to get their kids out of school. They insisted that by association, they didn't want to be a part of any of the demonstrations taking place. Whether from a lack of education, fear of harm, or losing their livelihood, these folks complied. No matter how hard their kids had worked to make it to college, their instinct to protect was greater than the potential freedom that came with an education and many demanded their children return home. My roommate was one of those men whose family insisted on his return, interrupting a promising opportunity, and possibly constricting the prospects for his life.

Then there was the other issue, the threat of imprisonment if we left the campus. Our choice was to be arrested and sent to jail or be expelled. State funded, the college was punitively expelling students gladly and easily. Once expelled, there were two options given; you were given no second chance to reapply, or you had to go through this rigorous re-admission process, which meant having a permission slip that could only be gotten from the president's office. If you didn't have one, you couldn't register. This fiasco was my first opportunity in showing audacity by taking part in meaningful actions of protest. One of my friends worked in the president's office and he would give me re-registration slips, which I in turn would distribute to friends on campus. This was an indelible moment for me. I was determined to give any student who had been expelled the opportunity to continue their education if they wanted to.

Today, as I look back on that decision to stand up against oppression, I see that it made an enormous difference in some lives. One was of a particularly good friend of mine. After years, our lives would once again cross in Atlanta. He'd often muse how his life would have been different had he been expelled. He'd also tell everyone and anyone who was ready to listen how I was the one who saved him from being expelled so that he could continue his education at Alabama State.

Coming full circle and looking back on my life, I see how the relationships, contacts, and actions I took helped me to become engaged in an important process that impacted the lives of others. These relationships in the future opened the doors to new opportunities, conversations, and ideas on exploring better ways for Black folks to exist.

The Emotional Scars of Violence

Despite the risks I took during these years of change, growth, and skill building, I was fortunate not to have any physical altercations with anyone. There are plenty of powerful stories of individuals who were not so fortunate, and who were willing to take the blows for freedom. One such is the late Congressman John Lewis who was beaten on the march over the Edmund Pettus Bridge from Selma to Montgomery. John Lewis went on to a political career first as a city council in Atlanta before moving on to Congress, to replace Andrew Young when he became the UN Ambassador. At the height of the Civil Rights movement Freedom Fighters faced many violent incidents, including what occurred on Bloody Sunday. The irony of the Civil Rights Movement was that it brought all of America together…every race on the side of Justice was represented in the Movement.

I tended not to be where the violence occurred. Whether it was intentional, pure luck or most likely because I was a student sequestered by the dictate to not leave campus, I skated by any form of violence and confrontation. However, I saw firsthand how the scars of violence seeped into everyday life. Houses being set on fire. Klan burning crosses in front yards. And this violence was not always limited to men either; women and children of these men were also targeted. Even my future wife, Leteria, had to deal with this. Her father was an active voice in the movement and a cross was found blazing in their yard. Those moments were so intense. The helplessness, the fear, the frustration came from knowing there was nothing you could do but make sure your loved ones were accounted for. In those moments of utter despair, we'd see people crying, praying, and then rising up, dusting themselves off to make the decision to either back down or keep moving forward. Very few in our community backed down. I was so blessed to have been with people who kept moving forward. It could not have been easy.

Peaceful resistance was key to opening up opportunities for change. On campus, our demonstrations were always peaceful and nonviolent because that's what Dr. Martin Luther King Jr.'s message was calling us to do. We did not initiate violence and we found ways to deal with those who were opposed to us without getting into physical altercations. Some movements like the Malcolm X Movement had a different message. These groups were not violent, per say, but sought Black empowerment through a different philosophy.

These days the lines are blurred between violence and nonviolence. The Black Lives Matters movement with social messaging against systemic racism started as a nonviolent one, demonstrating against the acquittal of George Zimmerman in Trayvon Martin's shooting death. As the message grew worldwide, gaining steam, it became more violent. Then the establishment responded with open season on Black males and females, resulting in the deaths of Michael Brown, Eric Gardner, Breonna Taylor, and George Floyd at the hands of vigilantes and police brutality. The hoods and burnt crosses were gone but the message was the same.

Today, the emotional scars of violence are still strong in Black communities. We rioted for Rodney King in Los Angeles, just as we cried out when 14 year old Emmett Till was lynched for violation of Jim Crow Laws in 1955. It is appropriate that three separate memorial will be erected for Emmett Till and an acknowledgement of our atrocious history in general but the establishment continues with its atrocities. It truly is too much to take, and it seems to have no end. These push backs when Black threaten the notion of white supremacy continues as an open war on Black males as have been spotlighted, such as Ahmaud Arbury

It isn't always easy to take a stand against injustice. It is even harder to do so without violence. Going head-to-head with someone who does not care if you live or die can be a life defining moment. So, when someone makes up their mind to give their lives for freedom, they'll never be the same again. Although much has been attributed to violence in

Black Communities, Black people are no more violent than any other groups. Black violence is more often the reaction to the pressure cooker of Black reality.

We've Endured So Much

The inalienable rights bestowed on every American by decree of the constitution seems to have left us out. Exercising our rights to Constitutional protection still seems to escape us and it has been anything but simple for the Black community. The notion that Blacks were considered two-thirds humans even with amendments of the laws post slavery has been hard to win. Today, the struggle for equality and our rights under the law may be better, thanks to some brave men and women of my generation, before and after, but it is far from complete. There is still so much work to be done. The sacrifices that have been endured to gain more freedom for a new generation is an honor and should be seen as such not as a cross to bear but as an unselfish act of our humanity. White America still has many tricks of the trade to suppress Black rising…from prison complexes to flooding communities with drugs, as was the legend of the 80's crack epidemic, which continues to decimate entire Black communities and even recently, the disbandment of Affirmative Action.

With this new rescinding of Affirmative Action, it is even more important to be educated today. It is more important than ever that we secede to positions of true power and impact. It's ok to be able to have a seat at the table and to be the voice of reason for centuries of behaviors that are hard to change but it is most imperative that we never give up the fight. There is a lot of talk about diversity and that's good, but inclusion means you have not only a seat but a voice at the table and equality means that voice at the table is heard and acted upon. Change, we all know, is one of the hardest things to take root but change must indeed be realized.

None of us were able to vote until the passage of the Voting Rights Act of 1965, but as we've learned having the right doesn't mean having the cooperation. Never clearer than in the 2017 election were the acts of blatant voter suppression. When it comes to voting rights there are still so many deterrents that work against the Black community. Even with a law you cannot change a heart for hatred; that is spiritual work that takes more time.

How do we deal with these constant setbacks in a way that help other people, while shaping a worthwhile legacy for our next generations? We continue to educate, inform, and demand equality. Even for me, with so many blessings, there is still a sense of distastefulness I face day-to-day. There are many days when I ask myself questions that need deep thought and spiritual guidance to resolve. Questions such as, how can my life impact others when I have still not gained equality in my own country? How can I influence others knowing the system and the structure will only allow them to get so far without pushback? How can I still live on purpose, with a spiritual base and be able to maneuver through this system that really was not designed for me? How can I make sure that those yet to come can benefit from my legacy? How can I keep going when at every corner new barriers are erected against my race?

I spent my days thinking about how to keep hope alive for those who may feel all hope is lost. The more I delved into my spirituality, the more I revisited what others have gone through as followers of Christ, and the more I gained strength. Historically people have been persecuted and denied rights because of their spiritual and cultural beliefs. So, I am going to stick by the belief that the entire concept of civil rights can come full circle and deliver the promised land. This is a long overdue delivery, outstanding to all minority groups in America facing racial prejudice.

Just recently, there was a hostage situation in my community in Sarasota, FL. Someone wanted to kill Jewish people because of their faith. I look at such acts against the Jewish community's continuing struggle to eliminate antisemitism as not only criminal, but cowardly. For every race that must spend energy fighting for inalienable rights it's debilitating and it's time lost in pursuing the best quality of life possible. Still, we must push forward in spite of these challenges.

Being engaged and working with others within our scope of abilities opens up opportunities for dialogue, understanding, and change. It is the right thing to do. We do not have to sacrifice rich life experiences, or the fun, friendships, and loyalty that can be a part of our diverse community. Unfortunately, the burden of progress falls to the under-represented and is a constant struggle.

Empowering Others Through Example

To me, going the distance is what we are about as a people. Our lives are a testament to this statement. We as elders who have lived through the worst of times are poised to equip others so they can move through life with ease. We also want the people we help to be inspired to help others do the same.

Back when the student movement arm of the civil rights movement was taking off, we were told many negative things. We were getting ahead of ourselves. We were second class citizens. We were inferior. We were not supposed to have the same rights, or the same access. Unfortunately, the psychological badgering and conditioning left some of us believing such unpalatable rhetoric. There is no question that we still suffering from the legacy of colonization and mental degradation but it is our job to eradicate it. It is time to know that we have been bamboozled and that now we have the power to do whatever is necessary to combat the unsavory conditioning of the past—not violently, but by becoming standout citizens who achieved our personal best.

Today, many non-negotiable Black people are viewed as a threat to the status quo and that is the big obstacle we are still trying to overcome. When we are educated, become empowered, run the race and do it better than most, we challenge the prevailing establishment and their notion of Black inferiority. Defying all the odds is great! So is dispelling this myth as we are continually upping the ante. Here we just need to look at athletes such as Tiger Woods, Michael Jordan, Serena Williams, and businesspeople such Michael Lee Chin, Reginald Lewis, Stephen A. Smith, Sheila Johnson, and entertainers Beyoncé, Jay Z, Oprah, and Tyler Perry.

One of my favorite success stories that firmly dispels this inferiority myth centers around Lonnie Johnson. Lonnie, an inventor, and scientist, grew up in Mobile. His most famous invention is the Super Soaker Toy Water Gun. With that invention and its patents, he became the number one toy seller in America for ten years. However, his story, like to many of our stories, started out quite differently. He was told in high school by a counselor that he should go to trade school and limit himself there. Had it not been for the council of family and friends and other people of influence in his life, he might have done just that. Instead, he went to Tuskegee University, where he earned two degrees, one of them in engineering. As you can see, the rest is history.

The blatant disregard for our abilities denied so many their rightful opportunities, especially if we accepted the premise that we were dreaming too big. Were it not for those who took a liking to us, or insisted that we press on, despite setbacks, many of us would never have risen to the level of achievement we have. If you look at the success stories of most strivers it often begins with a strong foundation at home, with parents or caregivers who emphasize the importance of education as an equalizer for opportunities. This is why I always revert to the importance of education and family.

TEACHABLE MOMENTS

There is great wisdom that can be absorbed by young people every day if they have access to it. In offering these types of insights through what I am sharing with you, it is my hope that you will see that you can have influence, and more so, you will be compelled to act differently in your own life. You are just required to do one thing—to dare for something better.

For you.

For your community.

For all.

Because we are all at our strongest when we are acting in the spirit of service and equality, finding a great mentor in service is a good place to start. This is where young Black minds can find their inner strength and resilience to achieve wonderful things in life. Whether you're an extraordinary chef and caterer like my friend Vincent or a future Secretary of Labor like Alexis became, you are a unique and treasured person in the making, being sculpted by your daily actions. This is why each day is a blessing that matters.

CHAPTER FOUR

FAILURE IS NOT PERMANENT

"The way you get meaning into your life is to devote yourself to loving others, devote yourself to your community around you, and devote yourself to creating something that gives you purpose and meaning."

—Mitch Albom

Civil Rights was creating change everywhere. The Little Rock Nine, a group of nine students who'd been enrolled in Little Rock Central High School, persevered as a result of the historic Thurgood Marshall led 1954 Brown vs. Board of Education lawsuit, in which he declared school segregation unconstitutional. Nine years later, in 1963, it gave me great pleasure when a significant person from my youth, a dear family friend, the late Vivian Malone Jones, integrated the University of Alabama. Behind me in school by a couple of years, she was one of the bravest human beings I have ever met.

When the University of Alabama was required to integrate, she wanted a spot at that school. As Vivian walked up to the university's entrance that first day in 1963, Governor George Wallace stood in the doorway between her and her education. She was escorted past him and into the building by the National Guard and police officers, per orders from US Attorney General Bobby Kennedy. Little did she know then that her future brother-in-law, Eric Holder would become the first African American US Attorney General. It's hard to imagine the trauma of this significant moment. She was isolated, received death threats, and was treated horribly by a lot of people. Yet, she was determined to withstand it all because it was the right thing to do. She had hopes and goals, and they could not stop her. She was the catalyst for integrated education for all Black students. I can only imagine the mental steel of the people on the front line who led this kind of change. What they must have endured could have driven many mad.

As the Civil Rights movement gained steam, not all freedom fighters advocated for peaceful protest. The electrifying Malcom X, a Muslim minister, human rights activist, and spokesman for the Nation of Islam had incredible charisma and did not advocate turning the other cheek. He preached a doctrine of Black self-reliance. He never encouraged starting riots but if riots started against us, he contended that we should respond in any way that protects us and by any means necessary. His national influence caught the attention of newsman Mike Wallace who did a documentary on him entitled, *The Hate That Hate Produced*, in which he explained why the revolution would not be a peaceful one.

I leaned into the doctrine of MLK's bridge building strategies which were more in line with who I was becoming. So, my time in Montgomery became a time of reflection, hope, and inspiration. The Civil Rights social and political peaceful movement that began in 1954 was opening new doors for Blacks but so was Malcolm's fiery rhetoric and demands, and I was living in a time of fruitful change.

Not everything was doom and gloom. During my two years on campus in Montgomery, Alabama I was very active. I went to parties, made a lot of friends and I met some of the most renowned people of the time, making friends with many who I still call friends. Among them are Randolph Thrower, LeBaron Taylor, Minnie Shelborne King, Thedora (Sweet) Thrower, Clinton Wright, Nellie Davis, Gerladine Mitchell Blackwell, Ivory Smith, and Alma Williams Kennedy.

It's Okay to have fun

High school was indeed wonderful and I had a lot of fun. It was there that I realized that having fun was a valuable part of life. There were as many wonderful times at Alabama State and I was fortunate that academics were never a problem for me. That meant I could focus on socialization and fun while not losing my edge academically. To be able to balance the two, like in high school, I followed a plan: I could spend time partying, and Alabama State was a party school, but, if I partied all night I'd spend all day in between classes at the library. I'd go there and take care of my assignments, study, and do all things academic-related. Young people today often find it hard to achieve that balance, but it is worth the pursuit and can lead to fun memories too.

The Graduate

I graduated from Alabama State in 1961 and returned to my roots in Mobile to teach social and health sciences at the middle school level. Back at home, there was a different energy in the air. The vibe of Mobile was fully expressing the resilience of its Black population. No stranger to blatant religious and color discrimination, Mobile even with the changing times, its prejudices were hard to suppress. Like America itself, Mobile was built on a caste system that put whites at the top, Blacks at the bottom and the many other races in between.

A city made up of a rich and diverse cultural population, like New Orleans, there is a high French influence. It went so far as to discriminate on the last name of a person! If you had a surname other than the more common Smith, Johnson, and so on, you could expect preferential treatment. Black and Eastern European mixed race people, French, Blacks from Africa and other lands of dark colored folks and Blacks who were born on American shores lived in Mobile and the darker-skinned folk bore the brunt of this discrimination. Overarchingly Catholic, religious discrimination against Protestants was also rampant. In Mobile, there was no shortage of discrimination about something. Mobile's rich, lustrous, and dark history is indeed intriguing.

47

The caste system was always in the forefront of every Black person's mind when I was growing up. Additionally, the intra-racial caste system it spawned meant that there was a distinct difference between the light-complected and the dark-complected Blacks. Common was the brown paper bag test, a new form of discrimination that was used by whites to exclude dark-skinned Blacks from certain opportunities by comparing their skin tone to the color of a brown paper bag. Regrettably, this kind of colorism was adopted in Black communities too. Those who were lighter than the paper bag were allowed into the prestigious clubs and organizations and those whose skin failed the test were rejected. Many light skinned Blacks even passed as white to gain access to positions of privilege. The effects of this psychological jerry rigging is still prevalent in today's Black society and has hampered the unity that will eventually be needed for full Black equality.

Friendships to Inspire

I grew up admiring the baseball legend Hank Aaron, who was also from Mobile. To me Hank was a good man and a warrior of higher calling. Hank endured a great deal of racism in his life, but it never stopped him from being kind and humble, or from becoming a great philanthropist. Because of social circles I moved in, I was later able to connect with the man I had admired for so long. Hank and I had an instant bond likely because we were both from Mobile and his humble beginnings mirrored mine. Always inspiring and a beacon of possibilities for many, he was admired around the world. Hank lived an extraordinary life, his impact a lasting legacy. I was enormously honored to have called him a family friend until his death in January 2021. His loss was tough to take.

It's hard not to mention the name of Alexis Herman (another Mobilean) when I talk about high impact people in the US, and specifically within the Black community. Alexis's mother, Mrs. Gloria Caponis, was my wife's, Leteria, third grade teacher and her father (Mr. Alex Herman) was the first King of Mardi Gras, a true mover and shaker not only in Mobile, but in the State of Alabama. He discovered and managed baseball legend Satchel Paige. Alexis also went on to become a Queen of Mardi Gras and attended Xavier University in New Orleans before returning to Mobile to find a job. Eventually she went on to become the first African American US Secretary of labor (23rd). Had she not had the fortitude to keep her own counsel, the system of discrimination could have altered her life.

Alexis' experiences give us insight into how life used to work for Black people back then, and how far too frequently it still is today. We were always advised to pursue low achieving roles and positions with low ceilings and low expectations. This is still a conversation I run into while mentoring. People like Dr. Gaines Thompson and Mrs. Valena Withers McCants, and many others who led the way to shattering ceilings and breaking down walls, empowered many of us to realize the potential of our beings. We were leaders and should not follow a system that was not favorably designed for people of color. I'd long held big expectations, and I'd long wanted to live up to my full potential. Being in close proximity to some of the movers and shakers of my time afforded me the opportunity to be with courageous people who walked their talk, were doing inspirational work, and who allowed me to work hand-in-hand with them. There were plenty of role models to emulate in my social group and I pray that those who come after me will have the same opportunities to meet stand out people.

I wanted to be a role model for the kids who came from my same humble beginnings. I wanted to say, "Hey, here's a Black kid, look at me. I did it so you can too." Now— I'm not a pull yourself up by your bootstraps kind of person, but I do believe that you can try to beat the odds—even when the odds can be stacked against you. I was ambitious, and I still had much to learn. But I'd already taken great strides to positively impact children who were in desperate need. Inspired to go even further, I wanted to move on to earn my Ed.D., but it was time to set my vision on that higher ground.

Integration

I loved teaching, but after four years of teaching, I resigned from my position as a middle school teacher because I wanted to teach at the college level. To do so, I would need an advanced degree. I'm sure it will

49

come as no surprise that when I originally applied to the University of Alabama, I was denied admission because Blacks were not accepted at that time. The denial still hurts, but I was determined not to let the color of my skin interfere with what I saw as my goal and purpose. Yes, I was in the segregated South, and if they wouldn't have me, I would find an alternative way to accomplish my dreams. I wanted a doctorate degree.

As a young Black man, I had been raised to feel that the only community that I could live in was a Black community, regardless of my societal status. Yet, I always sensed there could be something more for me; that my wingspan could be wider and extend beyond any boundaries or limitations imposed upon me based on my race. It was okay to have dreams like this and feel confident that you could achieve them but would something insidious interrupt that dream? I wasn't about to let fear or racism stop me. I felt I had a right to the American dream, and I packed my bags Indiana bound.

Indiana University, a top ten school, was 99.99% white. In an attempt to address the needs of diverse students, the federal government made grants available to white schools to recruit minorities. Indiana was one of the schools. By the time I was admitted, a handful of my friends had already been there, so I was well aware of the racial makeup of the school. These friends, however, had gone there as summer students when the campus was pretty deserted. I, on the other hand, would be a full time student, living on campus when the full roster of students were back. I was undaunted.

A public university with more people on one campus than I'd seen in my life, about eleven thousand during my era, was a major adjustment, and created a radical shift in my perspectives. The rigorous academic environment, being isolated from my culture and knowing I would never fully be accepted, although I was tolerated, meant that I had to go it alone. Very quickly, it became all too clear that I wasn't going to get to the same level of help as my white counterparts.

At that point, there were only a handful of full time Black people on campus. In fact, in all of my classes, I had one Black classmate, Doris Thompson. Doris was from Indianapolis and commuted daily.

She was a mature married lady who appreciated how challenging being away from home and being thrown into this unfamiliar environment in Bloomington must have been for me. She generously invited me to spend time with her family, which was a saving grace and eased some of my loneliness. Even with all the research and stories from friends, nothing could have prepared me for the experiences I would get at IU.

Being there yielded one revelation after another. My roommate was white. A married student from Indiana with a couple of children, he went home on weekends and we were passing ships. Being a social, I had to find my way into a wider social circle, and Doris's kindness helped me a great deal. Doris and Herbie introduced me to Indianapolis (Naptown), and it was an enjoyable experience. Their close friends included Mary and her husband Bob Smith. Through this couple I met Charles (Chuck) Rogers who was a graduate of IU and a Kappa Alpha Psi man. Chuck was a man around town and well connected.

IU, despite all the challenges, was an enriching environment and I got a lot of exposure to a much larger world. It was mine to experience as best as I could and to say I got the quintessential college experience is true. I would become a well-rounded person because of the culture of the school which exposed me to the arts! I fell in love with and still love to this day Arts and Culture. I was also a fan of the football and basketball games. And I was not short on entertainment! I got a chance to see artists I'd heard of, like Johnny Mathis and the Supremes. To see these larger than life entertainers of color perform to a largely white audience felt empowering. So, yes, IU opened up a world of exposure and I took advantage of everything I could. The funny thing is, although it was a totally different experience, I realized I already knew a lot of things because of Dr. Gaines Thompson, and it was not as intimidating as I thought it would be.

Truly, a key element in my survival at IU goes back to my mentor and friend, Dr. Gaines Thompson. It was because of him and my exposure to the Striker's Club that I was able to survive the social circles that existed at IU. Had he not taught me basic social graces, how to engage in politics, how to engage and learn from various cultures, it would not have been quite as easy to integrate or navigate these new surroundings. I was grateful to him when I realized that all his teachings were defining moments because, at IU, I had an opportunity to interface with students whose parents were very affluent, heads of organizations, CEOs, and the like. Their children talked casually about all their entitlements, and this offered me a different life perspective on the haves and have nots. It turns out, however, that while we can have different problems and different successes, we are all really just people trying to make our way to achieving the American dream.

After graduating from IU, I spent a year at the University of Southern Mississippi working on my doctorate. The University of Mississippi was a very, very different experience than Indiana. I could sense the South and the old familiar overt racism I was used to. Unlike IU, there were no mixed study sessions or working together. If you were Black you were on your own. It was while I was on that campus that Martin Luther King was assassinated. For me and many others the world stopped. I could not believe the courageous, gifted man had been gunned down. In a state of shock and a grief that felt too weighty, I left Mississippi and went home for a week to recalibrate in my Mobile cocoon.

When history is being made and you're in the midst of it, it's only life rolling along. In the eyes of the oppressor, by the 1970s Blacks were becoming too powerful and influential. Everywhere there were uprisings from people who were protesting America's misinformation about its Black citizens. Among them were Nina Simone. Her protest music, "Young Gifted and Black" was blazing the airwaves and became the anthem of Black Power. Malcolm X with his more revolutionary stance was more active with MLK having been murdered. The Black Panther Party, considered by J. Edgar Hoover as "the greatest threat to the internal security of the country," emerged as a visible representation of Black community. Angela Davis's alleged take-over of a courtroom in Marin County, California made the news. With each subversive, as labeled by the majority, a clarion call about the rise of a new Black consciousness was heralded. The establishment soon recognized that there was no turning back the clock Dr. King had wound up. Black America had found pride in who they were and donned dashikis, Afros, and berets to show support for the Revolution Party of the people.

The ironic thing is that America's competitive advantage comes from our multicultural society. Differences are what make us richer, and the more diverse, the better the outcome. The music, arts, culinary appreciation, and fashion we adopted are all imports from different cultures. It is my firm belief that America is only at the tip of its greatness, and when it finally realizes the enormous potential inherent in all its citizens, the promise of One Nation Under God, will be fully realized in glorious ways.

After a while it was time to enter the workforce again. I started sending out a new round of applications and got hired at Tuskegee—the very place I didn't want to go to college. I started there in June as an Assistant Professor in the School of Education. I taught Undergraduate classes in Psychology and graduate classes in Special Education. But Tuskegee was where God sent me this time because it is where I started dating my wife. It worked out well.

TEACHABLE MOMENTS

Young people today often find it hard to achieve balance, but it is worth the pursuit (and can lead to fun memories, too).

It is necessary to develop the introspection that will help you stand strong in the face of adversity. These senses are pride, courage, and confidence in facing the daily challenges we encounter as African Americans, and specifically African American men. Not allowing these challenges to interfere with who we are and how we deal with life experiences during our journey is a crucial step.

We all have challenges. Yours may be different from your white counterpart because we operate in a dual society. We need to explore ways to function and deal with all the challenges we face when you are a Black or part of a marginalized group. Recognize you cannot do this alone, and it works best when it is a part of a team, whether it is community support, relationships with mentors and family, or spiritual growth and guidance. All these things are defining moments that will either make us stronger or tear us down. When you have these moments, you must decide what to do with it and how to manage it.

What has happened with us and what earns the spotlight is, the continuous rise in crime and violence, in drugs, in the birth of illegitimate children, and the myriad health concerns we continue to have as a group. More focus needs to be placed on where we've succeeded in effectively lifting each other up through the support and encouragement of mentoring groups aligned with mitigating these risks. Get involved.

The challenges we face do not have to be crutches, leading to increased suicide rates because people cannot deal with the trials they face. People use drugs, alcohol, and sex to gain temporary comfort. However, these vices when they run out of control, lead to dire outcomes. There is a whole health crisis of not eating and sleeping and exercising and doing that which gives you a better chance of health. All of this ties together—especially as Black people.

My daughter Lailee was the one who helped me and the rest of the family drastically change our lifestyle, especially as it relates to the food we eat, the medicines we took, and the strain and stress on our bodies. In other words, we all have stressors; so how do we cope? Lailee's approach to wellness is what has helped me to shift how I cope and what I cope with. Instead of eating unhealthy foods and internalizing things that don't serve me, I learned to eat a basic plant-based diet, walk/run/or take a spinning class, and moderate what I consume It's time to evaluate your relationship with these things and see which path it is taking you down.

To combat what does not serve us, it helps to identify with what does. What does it take to survive? What do you do when you're faced with racism, lack of promotion and opportunity, and not offered access to that which makes everyone better? Is your response to stand tall in courage and continue to fight for your rights and do so in a peaceful non-threatening way? Or do you resort to domestic violence? Do you take out your anger and aggression on your spouse and children, or turn to drugs and alcohol and sex? Do you eat away your pain?

Finding healthy ways to cope with oppression doesn't resolve the issue on its own. However, it does offer a clearer perspective as to what you are up against. I want people to look and say, "Oh, here is this person that has gone through the same thing as me." Know that someone's experience can become your defining moment. This is a way to do better and not dwell on the negative sides of things, which are temporary. We are all connected. And every connection has an impact. For the people of Chickasaw Terrace, they understood that one small start toward helping to bring closure to the immense problem we faced outside our community, was to forge a spiritual connection with God—a willingness to lay down our burdens at his feet and seek answers through his teachings.

There can be great beauty in being "stuck together" in school. Developing lasting friendships, for example, which are more important than you could ever realize at the moment. Looking at your future, where you can talk to these people once a year and have a warm conversation that is meaningful. This makes a difference in terms of the expansion of friendship. This was especially true for me, who wanted to be both inclusive and engaging. I wanted people to be in my sphere but required that they be eager about their future and what they wished to achieve—not perfect, as none of us are, but eager for the opportunity.

CHAPTER FIVE

THE START OF OUR LIFELONG JOURNEY

*"The family is the foundation for love and
for maintaining spirituality."*

—Quentin L. Cook

Just as I was raised in love—something I wish everybody in this world could experience—I knew that moving on to my next stage and starting my own family, that love would need to be its foundation. This desire has been fulfilled and it has been amazing. It all began with a girl named Leteria.

Leteria: A Heart of Wisdom and Discernment a Love Meant to Be

You might have wondered why I haven't yet written more about my wife in the preceding chapters. That's because she deserves her own headline.

Leteria and I grew up in different neighborhoods but in the same community. I am six years her senior, which meant we ran in different circles and were not in the same peer group. We both understood the hardships of racism and came from homes where our families were very involved in the Civil Rights Movement. Our lives only crossed on Sundays as we went to the same church.

It was an immediate attraction for me when I met the adult Leteria and it was an added bonus that both Leteria and I came from families of service and faith. Her strong sense of spirituality was the glue that cemented the deal. It has guided us in all the stages of our marriage. I feel that being connected through faith and spirituality is a crucial element for all couples, and when challenges arise, what better place to find solace and solutions than in praying to God. Even before we were married, I saw how Leteria cared for me by how she pushed me to achieve. She was so graceful in accepting her role as the backbone of our new family, and a major supporter of all I've accomplished since meeting her.

When I started to date Leteria she was a new graduate from Tuskegee, teaching in Eufaula, Alabama, about an hour away. She'd often visit campus on the weekends to meet up with old friends and that's when our world intersected once again. We ran into each other at a social gathering, started a conversation, and we haven't stopped talking since. It became evident that as adults we were extremely interested in each other. I could tell we would be a great fit as we were so opposite, with her being reserved and with me being outgoing. It offered a wonderful balance to our developing romance.

Leteria's mother was a homemaker and her father the owner of a tree service business. Her parents were God-fearing and hardworking people. They lived on a street in Mobile where they had three or four houses, all next to each other, and all occupied by family members. Yes, they were a large, tight knit family. Leteria's sister, Joyce Stephens, is a teacher in the Mobile School System, her brothers Kermit, a Mobile Policeman and Melvin, Supervisor at Scott Paper Company. Her cousin, Marva Watkins, was also a teacher in the Mobile School System. Marva and I were very close because we were in high school together. She was two grades ahead of me and very popular on campus.

Leteria's father, like my Papa, was a staunch advocate and activist for the civil rights movement. People came to him for leadership, and he had the financial resources to become a leader of change. Because of that, her family got to experience the worst of human nature—visits from the Klan as they burned a cross in her yard, for example. This must have been so frightening for her family always having to be mindful

57

about their safety. So, though we weren't "friends," these were things I knew about her life before Leteria and I began dating. How ironic it was that the school I went to for two weeks was where I connected with my life partner. I loved the job, but I grew to love Leteria more…and I continue to love her more every day.

We began to date in September of 1968, and by the year's end I had proposed to her in Mobile. It was a surprise to her when I did that during Christmas. On June 7, 1969, she said "yes" to me at God's altar at the Antioch Baptist Church. It was the start of an incredible journey that is still going strong all these years later. We had a fabulous wedding at our church and held the wedding reception at the historic Battle House Hotel, as the very first African American couple who could do so—and it was a big deal. When we were growing up, this hotel was off limits to Blacks because of racism and segregation and the battle against integration that many white people supported.

When we got married, Leteria and I began working on our goals as a team. One of those goals was to get out of Tuskegee and establish new roots. We already had a vision for how our reach could extend outward. I also still wanted to get my doctorate degree, so we had big decisions to make and we were eager for what came next for us. As we get older, our age gap lessens in impact, but one thing never changes: the roots of our spiritual foundation. There is no doubt that because Leteria and I grew up in the same church, it helped us to bridge any gaps that might have been between us.

Ours is a life and marriage built on biblical principles, achievement, and a genuine love for each other. We don't always get along perfectly but we both know where we are going. Even in our marriage, we have benefited from the mentorship of significant people who understood the pressures couples fall under, especially when they are working toward great goals and opportunities. These people's guidance, friendship, and mentoring has meant the world to us.

The transition from being single into a partnership added immense value to who I was, and to my mission. I feel very strongly that God gave Leteria to me for that reason. We have done what most would expect, worked on things together and brought children into this world. However, it is our aligned philosophy that really makes us cohesive, despite such different personalities.

Rolling with When You're "At Odds"

With marriage comes disagreements. If you are being your authentic self, you are not going to have the same perspective and viewpoint on every matter. Embrace this, then navigate those rocky waters and find your solutions.

Leteria and I still disagree about things even after all these years. But our disagreements do not hold us back or place a wedge in our marriage. In situations where we are not in alignment, our disagreements become opportunities to express ourselves and reach an equitable decision: sometimes mine; sometimes a hybrid; but mostly hers because she is a fabulously smart and spiritual woman. When we disagree, we do three things: talk it through, pray on it, and deal with it.

These are the challenges of being married. You are not going to have complete agreement all the time. You are going to have your differences of opinion. Love and respect are key. The failure to nurture and value those two things are probably why today's marriages don't last the way they once did. You really see the dismal impact of this in single parent families in the Black community. Often it is a woman raising children and working full time. There is no engagement there, not by choice but in order to survive. There is little opportunity for the young children in these households to learn about good relationships, to absorb how they look and feel, and to mirror healthy ways to respond to disagreements.

Thankfully, despite our differences, Leteria and I always find our strength and resolve to be a positive force of good in this world. We are the only ones who can stop ourselves. Leteria's very presence helps serve as a reminder of this every day. She is a one-of-a-kind blessing—one who was uniquely designed to be my Coretta.

Finding the New Tuskegee

I wanted to get my Doctorate degree. Leteria wanted to earn her Master's. Together, we wanted to find out where to best do that so we began looking for a new place to start our lives together. We set out on an exploration to visit various parts of the country. Having grown up in the south, most other areas felt very foreign to us. We drove to Pittsburgh to visit Allegheny Community College and to interview. That trip also doubled up as our honeymoon. I still chuckle when I think about how thankful we were that our goals were exciting and romantic enough for us in those days.

North and Midwest territories, with integrated communities, were stark for us. For me, my only integrated experience was my time at Indiana University and Leteria had never experienced living in an integrated environment. However, when an opportunity to learn about a new community college prospect in suburban Chicago, we set out once again to explore. We had friends who lived there, so we had a place to stay while we checked it out. The community college was located in DuPage County, at that time, the fourth wealthiest county in the country. Its demographic was mostly fairly well-off white folks. You may be thinking that should have deterred us, but it was actually quite an appealing opportunity. This school was looking to diversify, and I was recruited by Earnest (Ernie) Gibson a Black gentleman who was a Tuskegee Institute alumnus. Naturally, I felt compelled to see what they had to offer and what type of life we could build if we lived there. Ernie assured me that both Leteria and I would have the opportunity to earn the advanced degrees we sought. The opportunity was so appealing, we decided to plant our roots, at least for a period of time. So, we moved to Illinois to teach in the suburbs at The College of DuPage, Glen Ellyn.

Back in America's heartland, the Midwest, I eased back into a white culture. I taught while I completed my Ed.D. at Northern Illinois University. In a similar fashion to my time at IU, I was fully cognizant that I needed to keep my authentic identity as a Black Man, and at the same time I needed to integrate with the white community. IU and Dr. Gaines Thompson had taught me well, and the options for a man of my times became more expansive because of my fluidity in cultural nuances.

That first Easter we were there was really shocking. It snowed! Coming from the south, we could not even fathom snow on an Easter Sunday. We were used to being outside for Easter, surrounded by flowers in full bloom. Now we were buried in snow.

The Foundation of our Legacy

The Gibson's took us into their world and guided us. They really played a role in our lives as a young married couple because they offered a positive model on which we could base our own marriage. They taught us how we could grow and mature as a couple. Additionally, they continued our education in social graces. The Gibson's entertained a lot and they advised us how to dress for each occasion, offering yet another moment in our growth. This is one of the reasons I cannot stress enough why role models are so important to today's youth.

Ernie Gibson and his wife Carolyn became close friends and valuable mentors to us. With their friendship and guidance, they were a significant part of our lives. In this whirlwind of positivity, our lives evolved into something more meaningful to our pursuits. As we looked to stabilize our living situation as a young married couple, they were instrumental in helping us get our first home. Finally, out of an apartment and living in a community, we settled into life. We also learned how to work better together and stay focused on what we wished to achieve. When there were challenges, we faced them head on.

As I noted earlier, I am the outgoing, gregarious, and social one. I'm the one who reaches out and forms relationships, both male and female. On the other hand, Leteria is more private, despite our public lives over the years. Some of the people I've met have since become long standing good friends of Leteria's but she is still the incredibly quiet one who is not only a good homemaker but a superb mother. In situations like this there are always adjustments to be made. Additionally, we were both used to being single and independent, and it took time to find the groove that would work for both of us.

At the core of our marriage—something that still exists to this day—is love. This is what makes it all work, and what makes the impossible become possible. The thing is, even though my parents were absent, I was raised with love and so was Leteria. So, we felt that love would keep us together through our challenges, regardless of what they were. And it has kept us together for fifty-four years.

I began working toward my doctorate and Leteria earned her master's. These were our individual goals and we supported each other wholeheartedly in achieving them. I was working at College of DuPage and growing into my professional self while undertaking my degree. I continued to ask the questions: How can I continue to serve? How can I make a difference in the lives of others?

Finding a Black community in our area was challenging but we did it because of who we were. While we were in the Chicago area our oldest daughter Lybra was born, and our goals extended even further. We now had someone to pass on all we had to give.

As I look back over these moments in our lives, I clearly see and recognize how we were able to achieve the harmony we were blessed with. We took on challenges head-on with trust, friendship, and integrity, understanding that we were a team on a journey to our collective fulfillment. This reinforces why our spiritual base has been so critical for us, as well.

You Always Need a Spiritual Home

When we first got to DuPage County, there was a pocket of the Black community close to the apartment we lived in, and they were native to this area. They all lived near each other and the whole community took up maybe two or three streets. There was a small Black church which we visited. But we didn't feel spiritually fulfilled there. Though the folks were Black they had their own northern culture. It felt strange to us. We knew we had to keep searching for a spiritual home that resonated with who we were.

The Gibsons went to an Episcopal Church and invited us to go with them on occasions. We accepted and really liked the service. Having grown up in Mobile, which is a Catholic-oriented city, we were familiar with Catholic customs. Mobile was so Catholic that no public schools even served meat on Fridays when we were young. We found that the Episcopalian church was a blend of Catholic and Protestant and that sat well with us. Because of the Gibsons, we switched from being Baptist to Episcopalians. Yes, it was a transition for us to become Episcopalian, but it felt necessary. We were trying to be spiritually fed and to grow as people, and we needed a home church. Today, both our daughters—Lybra and Lailee—are cradle Episcopalians. When I reflect on why we felt so comfortable there, I realize that the Episcopal church was made up of mostly like-minded individuals in the sense that people were functioning and operating at the same level. That was how it was designed to be.

I had joined the men's Bible group and we discussed Scripture all of the time. Their intellectual approach to finding God, rather than the fire and brimstone sermon of some preachers, worked well for me. Because we did not underestimate the earthly value of having a spiritual home and how that may impact you in your afterlife as well, we were glad to have found a spiritually uplifting place of worship.

I was also able to fulfill my personal service mission when I met Steve Knox and his family. Steve was a student at the College of DuPage, and I got to know him quite well. Growing up in white suburbia Steve had limited exposure to 'Blackness.' I recommended he transfer to Tennessee State University, a historically Black college in Nashville, to complete his bachelor's degree and truly embrace his roots. Today, Steve lives in Wheaton, Illinois, which is in DuPage County. Mentoring and advising him helped me to develop my passion for doing this for others. I mention him here because I have always felt my desire to mentor comes from my spiritual calling.

There were many wonderful moments and many friendships we cultivated along the way. We became friends with Joyce Carter and her husband Fred Carter who shared similar experiences growing up in the South. Joyce is a native Mobilean and Fred is from Hattiesburg, Mississippi. Both are graduates of Xavier University and still reside in Chicago. Joyce is a classical trained singer and has performed all over the country. Fred is a pharmacist. Although Fred is no longer with us, he left an indelible mark in the city of Chicago. Joyce is very close to us and is still actively engaged in the city.

I also had the great fortune to rekindle a high school friendship with Billy Williams and his wife Shirley. Billy is the Major League Baseball Hall of Famer who played for the Chicago Cubs. Through him, I had the pleasure of interfacing with Ernie Banks, Fergie Jenkins and many of the Cubs players and their families. Although Shirley is no longer with us, Billy and I are in constant contact today. Over the years, our friendships opened up many doorways to new friends, all people who had a desire to find their best selves in this world despite the world not freely offering them their fair opportunities. Knowing that I drank from the same water as these people, that we walked the same soil, brought a sense of pride. It also demonstrated how much power a community has to become their own catalyst for great and desired changes.

TEACHABLE MOMENTS

If you want a fuller picture of the world, then exposure to different cultures is absolutely imperative. The College of DuPage (COD) was my first experience teaching white students. Students at COD were mainly white and upper middle class, with a sprinkling of Black youth. The Black students primarily came from a small Black community in Wheaton, located in the heart of the DuPage community. These were working class people who valued education but had financial limitations. One of the Black students I mentored was Steve Knox. Steve was being channeled by the system to meet the stereotypical expectations they had for his demographic—sports—but he had the desire to achieve a different type of success. He was limited by his environment and of historical Black colleges and the opportunities they afforded much less the larger world. My experience outside that community meant that I was able to bring those options to the table. After much thought we, along with his parents, made a collective decision for him to go to Tennessee State University, a historically Black college, to complete his BS degree.

The first in his family to attend college, Steve became a teacher/program director in the Chicago Public Schools and later, the Assistant Football Coach and teacher at College of DuPage. He is married to Roberta, a speech therapist, and they have two sons. The first, Steven, went to Howard University; and the second, Jordan attended Morehouse College. Steve and I are very close friends today. Another major experience in DuPage County was meeting our neighbors Richard (Dick) and Barbara Winston. They became very close friends and role models for us as well. Dick was an executive with Eastman Kodak and Barbara was a typical suburban housewife in that she was a community volunteer, a soccer and baseball mom and was closely involved in her children's schools. They were great parents, nurturing four wonderful children. Richard Jr. is now an Attorney, Todd is a signature event planner, Karen (deceased) was a Marketing Specialist, and Randall is a major producer/director for ABC Shows and Netflix movies. We learned a lot from them and still remain close to all of the family.

In the 70's, the school itself was situated in various pods, with one of them being in downtown Chicago. In this pod, the city was used as the classroom. This meant you got a chance to experience what happened in downtown Chicago firsthand, rather than reading about it to gain secondhand experience. What was amazing about this is that it opened up a learning experience based on exposure; it was a school without walls concept. When the classroom becomes the environment around you the way you learn changes. Your observations are different and your intake on what you see shifts. It becomes more real than anything a book could ever offer. Students are given many opportunities to travel abroad in education, exactly because there is no way to replicate or substitute an actual lived experience in a traditional class-room. This is something you should seek to experience. Get as many firsthand experiences as you can, and that will provide you the chance to absorb the insights

It is necessary to develop senses that will help you stand strong in the face of adversity. These senses are pride, courage, and the confidence to face the daily challenges we encounter as African Americans and specifically African American men. It is crucial that these challenges should not interfere with who we are designed to be, and with how we deal with our experiences during this life's journey.

We all have challenges. Yours may be different from your white counterpart because we operate in a dual society. We need to explore ways to function when you are a minority. Recognize that you cannot do this alone, and that your best path to success will be as part of a team, whether it is community support, relationships with mentors and family, or the spiritual growth and guidance of your church fellowship. All these choices are defining moments that will either make you stronger or tear you down.

CHAPTER SIX

A LIFE OF SERVICE

"The way forward is the way back through"

—Buddha

Upon Reflection

There is, amazingly enough in this one America, quite a number of cultural differences between ethnic communities. But the truth is, everyone is trying to get to the same end goal—a happy and fulfilling life. Unfortunately, even today, we can't seem to accept others while retaining our own unique identity. I find it fascinating and helpful to learn about our differences in style, behavior, issues, concerns, and life strategies in general and I fully understand that the Black experience in America is unlike any other.

I cannot help but reflect on the world that I was born into, and what it meant to be intentionally disenfranchised by my homeland. Thankfully, my results were different from many of my high school classmates. Far too many dropped out of school and were lost or forgotten in the system. I never knew their outcome. I can only generalize from what I know of others, that life must have been hard for them. I still wonder, even now, how many got to achieve their goals and fulfill their happiness in this world?

To become a key person of service you need a lot of support, effort, and commitment to a greater vision than yourself. It takes not being afraid to be disliked by classmates who accuse you of reaching for too much or being "uppity" because you have clear and specific goals. When this happened to me I understood that my peers were operating through the lens of their personal experiences. I was able to ignore their comments as I continued to pursue my path of "there but for the grace of God." It isn't easy, and I have great sympathy for those who are susceptible to giving up over growing up with excitement for what life can offer.

I spent six fruitful years in Illinois where my oldest daughter Lybra was born in 1973. Then, in June of 1973, at the age of thirty-three, I completed my Doctorate in Education and new opportunities opened up for me. At first, it seemed like the next step would take us to San Francisco. I had applied for a job at a community college there and received an offer. Then by chance, I got a call from a colleague at the College of DuPage, who shared with me that a two-year state college in Atlanta, a part of the George State University system, was opening and looking for administrators and staff. While San Francisco was a great opportunity, it was also thousands of miles away from friends and family in Mobile. Atlanta was hours away, so it became the choice, and it did work out. I received the opportunity, and it was the onset of a new wave of inspiration. To say it was a blessing to be headed back south to Atlanta was an understatement.

Arriving in Atlanta

I was already familiar with Atlanta as a visitor, but living there was new, exciting, and just fantastic. I saw so many Blacks who were thriving in its robust environment and the possibilities seemed endless. Additionally, Atlanta had the largest consortium of historically Black colleges and universities right there in downtown Atlanta. This included Morehouse, Spelman College, Clark Atlanta University, Morris Brown, Atlanta University, and Morehouse School of Medicine. These rich educational opportunities obviously appealed to me.

Being in the academic and physical presence of some of the greatest men who ever lived was exciting. Dr. Martin Luther King Jr. went to school at Morehouse. So too did Maynard Jackson, the first African American mayor of Atlanta. The all-women's college, Spelman College, produced outstanding women like Marian Wright Edelman and Alice Walker—and my two daughters. Socially, this made Atlanta a good place to be, while the buzzing, vibrant atmosphere of the city made it a good place to raise a family. I was energized by what Atlanta could bring and it all started with my new job.

About twenty-five of us were hired to help open this new college, which was in downtown Atlanta. One of the people who was a part of this effort was Jean Childs Young, who was Ambassador Andrew Young's wife. It is a point of distinction that Andrew Young was the first African American US Congressman from the South. Jean and Andy befriended us and our one-year-old Lybra, right away. They also had a one-year-old son, Bo, and three older daughters. Through their friendship and connections, we were introduced to Atlanta. This is another reason why I say that the people we build connections with matters, when there is a difference to be made. For example, Alexis Herman also lived in the Atlanta area when we moved. Shortly after, she moved to Washington, D.C. as part of the transition team of President Jimmy Carter and became head of the Women's Bureau in the Department of Labor. As I've shared, in time she would become the US Secretary of Labor.

Seeing all of these connections come to light was stimulating and inspiring. It was in Atlanta, if I had ever been uncertain, that I categorically knew that I was fulfilling my calling which was to make a difference in others' lives, particularly people of color. I took my experience as a mentee of Dr. Thompson and decided to become a mentor for those to whom I could be of service. I couldn't help but be drawn to young people who are facing the same issues that I faced—or those that had it even worse. I felt and still feel called to extend a helping hand. With the splintering of close knit Black communities, choosing the path of service is an ever pressing need today.

In this role, I learned the importance of financial support for our Black community—which I knew we needed in order to achieve any measure of success. I started to volunteer more and became involved in a circle of friends who valued community, spirituality, uplighting our people, and driving change. Leteria and I gradually became a part of a new world.

Atlanta: A Mecca

Community is about Investing in People: The Power of Influence

Atlanta is in the South, but by 1974 with the election of its first Black Mayor, Maynard Jackson (followed in 1992 by Andrew Young), it was moving at lightning speed to create real opportunities for Black folks. Four years into my career I was meeting and interacting with many influencers who would further impact my life, and who offered me the opportunity to help build a city that would become a Mecca for Black folks. Richard and Diane Greene were some of the first people we met upon arrival. Richard was CEO, Southwest Community Hospital and Diane, a community volunteer, and Mental Health Professional, quickly became friends. Both retired, they live in Brooklyn, New York. They are world travelers and art collectors. Margaret Crawford Howell introduced us to the city and a host of new relationships and friends. Margaret and her daughter are an integral part of our family.

One of my best friends in high school was Vincent Warren Henderson. Vincent moved to Washington D.C. and became an extraordinary chef, which was his passion and his hallmark. He rose to great prominence as an international master chef by becoming the caterer of choice for White House events during the Clinton administration. Vincent was extraordinary in his craft. In fact, Vincent became one of the first Black sous chefs to work in Boston at the Harvard Club in the 1960s. Vincent was responsible for all of Alexis Herman's events when she was in the West Wing of The White House before she became Secretary of Labor. He also did high-profile events for numerous key political people, including

Dorothy Height of the National Council of Negro Women in the D.C. area. His business spread to New Orleans, Birmingham, Atlanta, and our hometown of Mobile.

Back in the day, Vincent had the same mentor I did—Dr. Gaines Thompson. When we graduated from high school, he opted to go to Fisk University in Nashville and our paths went separate ways. But, many years later we were able to rekindle our friendship at the funeral of Dr. Gaines Thompson. I was living in Atlanta at that time and as fate would have it, Vincent worked for a restaurant chain with its main office in Atlanta. When he finally transferred to Atlanta, I was lucky enough to have him as the caterer for all of my events, which included ones for Ambassador Andrew Young, Vivian Malone Jones, Maynard Jackson, and other notables. He even did our daughters' sweet sixteen parties. Vincent was the chef for our Christmas Evening tradition which started out as a small affair and grew into one of the major events in our community. Vincent passed away about ten years ago, and, it was devastating to my family, and all of our friends. He had become so much a part of all of our lives. Whenever he was in town, people would travel from across the city just to eat one of Vincent's newest creations! Hailed from Mobile with Creole influence he wasn't just a chef, his larger than life personality was what made every meal a celebration. It was not a meal if Vincent wasn't in the kitchen with a glass of Crown Royal in his hand. People like Vincent, who everyone should surround themselves with, was indeed the real deal. To commemorate his passing, we pulled together all of his recipes that he'd published. Because if it isn't Vincent's gumbo, I don't think I can eat it.

Diverse people with skills, passions, talents, and memorable personalities were part of the circle I navigated once we arrived in Atlanta. For example, Vincent introduced us to a white gay couple —Jim and Jerry—who lived downtown Atlanta and next door to Vincent and his then wife Jennifer. Growing up in Mobile, I don't know that I would have ever been exposed to a liberal gay white male couple. In fact, my daughters grew up knowing "Jim and Jerry"—without even a concept of understanding or caring about "gay." Jim and Jerry were the hottest couple around in Atlanta. They were fashionable, held extravagant parties, and introduced us to people and experiences that we would have never had—whether it was in the arts or music. As I've grown in wisdom and reconnected with many, I appreciate more than ever the many people who started off at my high school, who survived and thrived through their journey, and who became people of influence as adults. All helped to expand my circle of friends and experiences.

Such is the case with Hal and Alice Wyatt, a couple we met in DuPage County, who had recently moved to Atlanta and to our surprise appeared at Lybra's Debutante Cotillion sponsored by The Links, Inc. After ten years, we renewed our friendship and today maintain a close relationship. Hal was with IBM and Alice a Reading Specialist. Hal became very active in the 100 Black Men of Atlanta and Alice the AKA's. We worked on any number of community focus initiatives and charitable causes. After retirement, they moved to Plano, Texas to be near their daughter Nicole.

My Call to Action

Meeting so many people and getting to know the story behind each of them was a delightful experience. From what I could tell, people who invested in others connected with them in ways that broke down the walls that divide us. That is only logical, I suppose, and it is a reason that when one has a biblical mandate to lift others up, it should be taken seriously.

Meeting Mrs. Coretta Scott King was a powerful experience for me, and I did not hesitate to get involved in her work. After her husband's death she founded The King Center, continuing his work in civil rights activism as a social justice advocate. I had to be a part of this work. MLK's significance in the civil rights movement had already benefited me, and it was time to give back. Working with Mrs. King, as well as with Mrs. Christine King Farris (MLK Jr. 's sister) to solidify his legacy was a most gratifying experience. Her tireless work was instrumental in leading the charge to get a federal holiday named after Martin Luther

King, Jr. on his birthday. And lest we forget, this special day continues to keep his work alive with the massive annual celebration we hold each year in his honor. It was Mrs. Christine King Farris who introduced me to the then new minister at Ebenezer Baptist Church (Rev. Dr. Rapheal Warnock). I was told to assist him in any way possible in maneuvering throughout Atlanta. I immediately took heed and recommended him for membership in the 100 Black Men of Atlanta. Little did we know that this young and vibrant minister would become the first African American US Senator of Georgia. Mrs. Christine King Farris recently passed and she was honored and memorized by the Spelman College, City of Atlanta, and the State of Georgia.

Change in policies might not solve all the issues we face as a nation but politics should be important to everyone. Political impact on policy makers who enact changes in the law is significant for our community in ways both large and small. One of the campaigns I worked on was for Maynard Jackson, Atlanta's first Black mayor. Maynard was completing his first term when we arrived. He had chosen to run again, and I became involved in the mayoral races. I was also involved in Andrew Young's campaign for the mayorship, as well as the one which followed for Shirley Franklin, who went on to become the first African American woman to be mayor. The art of politics is such that one hone skills in negotiation, collaboration and trust building, all invaluable assets to a change agent.

Politics was an effective tool for those who had the ability to influence others to new ways of thinking, acting, and responding to the process of change. Hank Aaron was one such person. I have to single out Hank Aaron and his wife Billye for their work as philanthropists and community builders. Their example was, to me, a constant reminder of giving back, and the epitome of the concept of "to whom much is given, much is expected." Their heart and ability to connect with vulnerable people was powerful for me to witness. The day the world lost Hank Aaron they lost more than a baseball great, they lost a mighty difference maker who was committed to helping those in need. Perhaps his most unheralded legacy, and possibly his most powerful, were the fruits of his giving heart. His spouse and love of his life, Billye Suber Aaron is the epitome of social graces, and was a true partner in supporting his philanthropic efforts.

Considered one of the greatest baseball players of all time, Aaron was the baseball legend who broke Babe Ruth's hallowed mark of 714 home runs, finishing his career with numerous big league records. Hank and his wife Billye are who I consider change agents for a cause. A fellow Mobilian, he withstood severe racism throughout his career yet never folded under the pressure. He was a true inspiration and role model for all. Through the Aarons' dedication to important causes, and their outstanding ability as fundraisers I really began to blossom into someone who could make a difference because I learned many rules of engagement around fundraising from them. Leteria and I became active in several key organizations in the city. She was active in Jack and Jill and was a charter member of the Dogwood Chapter of The Links.

Thanks to Clarence Williamson, a great friend, I joined the Alpha Phi Alpha Fraternity and through Nathaniel Goldston was introduced to The 100 Black Men of America. This civic organization aims to educate and empower African American children and teens and to improve the quality of life within communities of color by enhancing educational and economic opportunities for all African Americans. The organization's motto of "real men giving real-time" and also "what they see is what they'll be," embodied everything I was about. I became a founding member of the 100 Black Men of Atlanta chapter, under the leadership of Nathaniel Goldston, an astute and successful businessman. Goldston used his business, political, civic, and philanthropic savvy to grow the organization by recruiting successful Black men in every field to become members. There were nineteen founding members. An invitation-only organization, it was not meant to be exclusionary, but rather wanted to attract people with the same vision and aspirations of success and desire to give back.

Our members took on the task of transforming the lives of severely at-risk youth from what was considered one of the lowest academic achievement public school in Atlanta—Archer High School (Gladys

Knight is a graduate). This school had a dropout rate of 60+ percent and we made a commitment to those kids to do all we could to impact their lives in positive ways. Later, we adopted an 8th grade class of thirty-five students and promised that any student who graduated would have their college education fully funded by us at any university in the country. The 100 Black Men was flush with outstanding mentors. All the Black mayors of Atlanta were in the organization, except for the two women mayors—Shirley Franklin and Keisha Lance-Bottoms. We boasted Presidents of the historically Black colleges and universities (HBCUs), CEOs, doctors, lawyers, educators, US congressmen and businessmen, all dedicated to doing the work to combat the remnants of inequality in our communities.

It was a responsibility that was not taken lightly, and the joy of seeing students succeed brought us so much more than we could have imagined. Seeing change unfold is a blessing that is hard to describe in words. For me, knowing that my hard work was benefiting someone else's life brought me to a place of spiritual completion.

We pretty much adopted these kids and it became a family affair. My mentee was an 8th grade female, Pamela Lewis, from Perry Homes, which was a high-risk community close to where Archer High School was located, in northwest Atlanta. Our entire family was dedicated to helping those who did not have the same benefits we had and with Pamela, one of the students, Leteria stood side-by-side with me in this effort. My whole family took Pamela in, and she basically became our third daughter. We spent weekends with her, and we took her to all the cultural and social justice events we participated in. When she graduated from high school with honors, she was accepted into Hampton University, which is an HBCU in Hampton, Virginia. After Pamela graduated from Hampton, she began teaching in the Atlanta public schools, where she became Teacher of the Year. What a wonderful success story! Helping others keeps me grounded in the aspects of life that matter most.

Another organization that was doing good work was the United Negro College Fund. One thing you'll learn is that change requires not only effort but the kinds of funds that can ensure the success of the programs implemented to accomplish their desired outcome. That meant I had to become an astute fundraiser. Participating in Billye Aaron's fundraising efforts to support the UNCF mission was another amazing experience. The results of our fundraising efforts were impressive, with events like the Mayor's Masked Ball, raising millions of dollars for the organization over the years. Year after year, it took enormously talented people taking massive action and doing hard work to pull off this Mardi Gras style event. I loved being a part of that type of energy and I loved black tie events.

It was during this time that I met Ralph and Leita Hughes. Ralph was the first African Americans General Manager of Rich's Department Store in Atlanta. We became very good friends, and he went on to become the Vice President for Marshall Fields, and subsequently Macy's in Chicago. In Atlanta, he became a member of 100 Black Men. Ralph was a key contributor to our large-scale events. He recognized that no one goes it alone, and giving back to a community that supported his mission was the right thing to do. Like me, he now lives in Sarasota, Florida.

People willing to assist and become involved are all around you; your workplace, in your social groups, among your mentors, and in those who you befriend. As time went on in Atlanta, I was able to grow my career by being of service. The people I met professionally became the same people who helped my efforts to fundraise for causes that mattered greatly to me, which tended to evolve around the challenges facing the Black community.

Along the way, my efforts were helped along by Woodrow (Woody) Hall, Ernest Lamont Greer, and William Cooper. Woody is an entrepreneur who has contributed so much to the growth and development of Atlanta. Recently, he put his life on hold to take care of his ailing wife, Dr. Glennda Hall and father, Dr. Clyde Hall. Ernest is Co-President, of Greenberg Taurig Law Firm. He and his spouse Patrice are major donors and contributors to the city of Atlanta. William Cooper is a Cardiovascular Surgeon and he and his spouse, Sandy are actively engaged in the Atlanta community giving their time, talent, and resources to the city of Atlanta. They all became friends of long standing and together we each of us have been called to serve in our own unique way. Although I don't see them as often as I would like, we are still good friends today.

Expanding on Opportunities

My time at Atlanta Junior College (now Atlanta Metropolitan State College) was beneficial and helped me, so to speak, get my feet in the door. While there, I was selected to join the 1986-87 class of Leadership Atlanta. What an awesome experience. I was the direct beneficiary of many of the people I met, and my next opportunity came at the recommendation of Dr. Douglas Greenwell, who was head of the Department of Family and Children Service for the state of Georgia. I was recruited to work for Morehouse School of Medicine (MSM) as Head, for the Center of Child Abuse and Neglect, for one year. Later, I became an Associate Vice President and the Executive Director for External Affairs and Development. I found a home that was able to give me opportunities to practice all the skills I had been developing. My fundraising work was, by nature, closely tied to my roles at Morehouse. I served six presidents in the twenty-five years I was there. They are Dr. Louis Sullivan, the founder, Dr. James Goodman, Dr. James Gavin, Dr. David Satcher, Dr. John Maupin, and Dr. Valerie Montgomery Rice, the first female President of MSM. Dr. Douglas and his wife Billie were quite significant to my family, both personally and professionally. They were door openers and friend makers. In fact, they are the godparents to my youngest daughter, Lailee.

Being well-connected helped me to expand on new relationships and opportunities. I was able to develop substantial contacts and bring those resources and relationships to MSM. Since I basically represented the institution to the community, and that was a task I took seriously, I was able to significantly grow our reputation and funding. From a political perspective I was well versed and engaged in that arena. Knowing politics mattered and understanding the nuances of fundraising mattered too. I knew, based upon my prior fundraising work for worthy causes, that I had a knack for those things. All this solidified my purpose of helping and serving others.

This brings me back to the work of the 100 Black Men of Atlanta. Remember, we were committed to getting these kids in the impoverished, underperforming high school to not only graduate, but go on to college at our expense. We expected that this would take about $365,000 a year to do if we had the success we were determined to have. We didn't personally have that type of capital to self-fund, so we needed to explore fundraising opportunities. I was excited to head up that initiative.

I organized a black-tie event and coined it *Le Cabaret, Le Cabaret, Le Cabaret*, as a benefit for our featured program 'Project Success'. It became the signature black-tie event in the City of Atlanta. The 100's was the first to do this and it was of huge success. It took a lot of work and a lot of money to coordinate. The money came in the form of corporate sponsors whose philanthropic mission matched our own and included, The Coca Cola Company, Delta Airlines, UPS, Bank of America, Georgia Power Company, and The Home Depot.

In order to attract people to the event we needed to do something special and out of the ordinary. We were the first organization to have big name entertainment at the World Congress Center. Our headliners included Phyllis Hyman, Gladys Knight, the Four Tops, The O'Jays, Jeffery Osbourne, The Whispers, Ashford and Simpson, The Temptations, Frankie Beverly and Maze, Chaka Khan, and Stephanie Mills, and the list goes on. Along with our sponsors, these nationally known entertainers drew in enough fans to make a real financial difference to the children we had adopted. We even made the society pages in *The Atlanta Journal Constitution*, something that was still kind of rare for an organization that supported Black people within the community. To this day the event name remains the same. My wingspan covered many organizations and being a founding member of the Atlanta 100 Black Men chapter, I am most proud of this accomplishment, and that the projects I became involved in there that are still foundational to the organization

Each year, and now in its 37th year, the 100's invited famous keynote speakers to their Annual Luncheon to address the Project Success students and community. Colin Powell, before he became Secretary of State, was stationed at Fort McPherson in Atlanta. He was a featured speaker at the 100 Black Men of Atlanta luncheon honoring our Project Success students. He was so impressed with our mentoring program that when he became Secretary of State and began the American Promise Program, he referenced the Project Success Program as a model. It was at that luncheon where Colin Powell spoke that the President and President-Elect of the100 Black Men of Atlanta were sworn in by Robert Benham, the first Black to serve as Chief Justice, Georgia Supreme Court, and Leah Ward, the first Black female Chief Justice of Georgia Supreme Court.

We were equally grateful to speakers such as Alex Hailey (author of *Roots*), Congressman John Lewis (a member), Congressman David Scott (a member), Judge Glenda Hatchett, all empowered the students with their presence. Attendees at the luncheon were particularly moved when Judge Hatchett delivered an impassioned speech about getting to a better America, a better life for ourselves, and hope for future generations. There were also entertainers Jennifer Holliday and Kathleen Bertrand who made the events so special. I was proud to be recognized on the pages of magazines for the stellar work the 100's were doing and to stand tall in pictures with various people of affluence who gave their time to such a worthwhile cause. Reflecting on the key things which created change and that helped the city of Atlanta to grow, I am humbled and pleased that I was a part of all that.

Our Christmas celebrations were exceptional and the highlight of our holiday season. At one celebration we were thrilled to have the 43rd President of the United States, Bill Clinton, as a guest, along with Jennifer Holliday. Modestly speaking, I must say that during my term as Chair of the Social Committee, my team of dedicated members and I really made special things happen and our guests really looked forward to this event. And it was all due to our supporters. Finding success in these fundraising efforts comes back to the simple act of sincerely nurturing the relationships I had developed, and I had a lot of connections and support from the various organizations I served in. Today, the 100 Black Men of Atlanta continues to thrive and keep the legacy going, under the leadership of Sidney Barron, Chair, Board of Directors and Aaron Swan, Chair Elect. Sid and I have developed a long standing relationship and we are in constant contact. Aaron is my adopted nephew and extended family member.

I was able to bring many of these resources not only to Morehouse School of Medicine, but also to the nonprofits and other charitable efforts I was involved in. Because of all of the charities I supported, I had established strong relationships with the hospitality industry and knew, and still know, all the GMs at key hotels such as the Ritz Carlton, St. Regis, Four Seasons, Hyatt, Intercontinental, and Omni. Niles Harris was one of these men. He was the first Black General Manager of a major hotel in Atlanta. I introduced him to the 100 Black Men of Atlanta and he replaced me as Chair, Special Events. Currently, he is the Managing Director and Vice President of Operations for the Highgate Hotels in New York City. He and his wife Jean became good friends and I maintain the relationship, even today from Florida.

It was also a pleasure to develop a close friendship with Xernona Clayton, Founder of The Trumpet Awards. This social event afforded me the opportunity to interface with many notables including First Lady Michelle Obama. I still stand in awe of meeting Lena Horn, Sidney Poitier, Diahann Carroll, Harry Belafonte, Sammy Davis, Jr., Cicely Tyson, and Nancy Wilson.

All the efforts made to get to know people not only for the help they offered, but as people I genuinely cared about, meshed all my worlds into one large resource that benefited the Morehouse School of Medicine, the 100's, the Church of the Incarnation where Leteria and I were members under the leadership of Father Rick Brittain, as well as to St. Paul's Episcopal Church with Father Robert Wright as our Rector. Robert Wright is currently the first African American Bishop of the Dioceses of Atlanta Episcopal Churches. Bishop Wright and his wife Dr. Beth Sara Wright remain dear friends. In fact, immediately upon relocating to Sarasota, Bishop Wright called Father Fred Robinson, the Rector at Church of the Redeemer of Sarasota, for an introduction. Once Father Wright became Bishop Wright, Rev. Charles Fischer, the Assistant Rector, became Rector at St. Paul. I had known Father Fischer over the years when he was a student at Morehouse College. He and my youngest daughter, Lailee, are very good friends going back to their Morehouse/Spelman days. I had the pleasure of serving Father Fischer and his wife Rhonda during their stay at St, Paul. They are now in Pittsburgh, Pennsylvania continuing their ministry with their two sons. Father Fisher and I still maintain a close relationship today.

A great way to explain how these relationships are built and remain intact is to use the analogy of the home. When we have a home, we maintain it with the paintings on the walls, the gardens outside, and the interior furnishings. This is called maintenance, and it carries over to friendships as well. Friendships need to be continuously nurtured and developed in order to stay vibrant. If more people did this type of people nurturing, think about what potential could exist. It would make a powerful difference, I am certain. It is worth the effort and investment; it truly is.

What I have been able to give is as a result of my social connections and ability to maintain good relationships are things I'd learned back in Chickasaw Terrace. My entire Mobile experience—the environment I grew up in, the church as the cornerstone of family were steppingstones to my future. Today, I belong to a different faith with different customs, but it is still the church where meaningful relationships can transform. It takes an investment of time to cultivate relationships of trust and respect. It does not happen without effort, and because relationships are key to what I do, I could have accomplished nothing without them.

A Few Words About Service

People have often asked about my intense desire for service. I've always had the desire, dating back to Papa's influence. My desire was nurtured by family mentors, church family, and by others who reached out to helped me. Helping others was something that I needed to do as well, and so that's how I have structured my life. Living in Atlanta gave me the platform to do that. All of the organizations and situations there provided an opportunity for me to serve, and to give back and I embraced them fully, across the board, always looking for ways to enrich others' lives through my skills and abilities.

Other Influential Influences

Atlanta became a pivotal move to my dream. I was beginning to understand that no matter where I lived or traveled, I was getting there because of the people in my life. My mentors were part of this continuum. People like Papa, Aunt Catherine, family members, Ministers and Deacons in the church and community members, Mrs. Valena Withers McCants, and Dr. Gaines Thomas were individuals I looked up to as a child, who profoundly shaped my life. They had so much knowledge to share, and hearts filled with servitude to inspire. Then there were those who came after me, such as Alexis Herman, Vivian Malone Jones, as well as her sister, Dr. Sharon Malone, who happens to be married to another influential person of color—former Attorney General of the United States, Eric Holder. I'd always wanted the best and Atlanta proved to be the right choice…I could live and do as I saw fit relative to my life and dreams.

Over the years, our friendships opened up many doorways to new friends, all people who had a desire to find their best selves in this world despite the world not freely offering them their fair opportunities. It also demonstrated how much power a community has to become their own catalyst for great and desired changes.

My appreciation for my Alabama roots is deep, but it does not begin to compare to the opportunities Atlanta afforded. Atlanta was and is rife with influential and impressive Black people and to my fortune I met many of them: Coretta Scott King and her family, Ambassador Andrew Young and his family and the great Maya Angelou, who became an advisor of mine and who bestowed on my family great wisdom. How we enjoyed our visits to her homes (Winston Salem, North Carolina, and Harlem Morris Park Historic District) where she would cook for us, as we reminisced about life. She was a 'Phenomenal Woman.' Her words of wisdom will always be remembered. These people were at the top of their game in their respective fields and each had audacious goals. They were disciplined and committed to finding success. But more important to me was that they were equally committed to improving the world around them and in pursuing equality for all. Every one of them inspired me to dream even bigger as they went on to blaze trails throughout the world. Their new zenith, of course, was cause for more institutional ostracization but as I said choices are to be made.

My journey has not been without its ups and downs and reconsiderations. When disappointment came my way, I had to decide, how do I manage it. That was always the biggest question that I needed to find the answer to as I grew into a young man navigating high school and then college and then adulthood. Not everything went the way I wanted it to. I was very disappointed when I did not get the Presidency of Alabama State University and Talladega College.

Oftentimes I was impatient and wanted things immediately. When that happened, I needed to find an effective way to respond that wouldn't lead to my digressing in any manner. I had too much I wanted to get done. My faith never wavered, and it was what kept me rooted when I'd put my trust in some person or some situation and it didn't work out. When trust is breached it is always frustrating and disappointing. And to some without the proper guidance, it sadly becomes expected.

I know you've heard the saying, if you are living on purpose, you'll never work a day in your life. As I look back over my life, the defining moments of truly understanding who I was and getting clear on my purpose are linked to the spiritual component of my life, which has proven itself to be the most relevant. I was growing into who God had designed me to be and was joyfully dedicated to fulfilling my plan according to his design. Even on the frustrating and downtrodden days, which were many, I knew I was on the right path. These challenges helped me understand that attainment comes with its share of disappointments, but pressure makes diamonds.

TEACHABLE MOMENTS

We live in a world where everything requires maintenance. We work hard to maintain our jobs, our house, our finances, and our relationship with God. But the one area that is often overlooked is the maintenance it takes to keep a friendship strong. Strong friendships are hard for some people to achieve. How many will be able to say they are friends at age eighty with someone they first met at age five? It's wonderful to be friends with people who have known who you are for your entire life. They know where you came from, and what you've done. I'm such a strong proponent of keeping connections intact, I still reach out to people and connect. Many people don't do this today and it is creating gaps between us that are harder to bridge. I don't want my design to be so unique that I'm the only one who does this. Everyone should find a way to establish these connections in life.

Me in elementary school.

Mobile County Training School graduation picture, 1957.

Our engagement made the Mobile Newspaper…Pictured Leteria.

Our Wedding on June 7, 1969, Mobile, Alabama.

Educator **Willie Clemons** said he'd like to get Robert Daskal's bold graphic design painted by hand in fashion's newest shades. The silk tie is $67.50 at Saks Fifth Avenue.

Article in *The Atlanta Journal Constitution*.

With our cousin Marva Watkins in Tennessee.

Speaking at the Community College Conference.

Our annual holiday party with Walter Young (left) Joyce Dennis,
me and Sonjia Young.

Jean Young (front row, second left) was the wife of Ambassador Andrew
Young. We were with the Foundation Board of Atlanta Junior College
(now Atlanta Metropolitan State College).

Leteria and I hosted the Egyptian Delegation to the US, 1975/1976.

Former Presidents of Morehouse School of Medicine
Dr. John Maupin (l) and Dr. James Gavin (r) .

At the 100 Black Men of Atlanta's signature event
- Le Cabaret, Le Cabaret, Le Cabaret.

At the 100 Black Men of Atlanta's signature event Le Cabaret,
Le Cabaret, Le Cabaret.

Me promising I would not singing…Ah well.

Leteria and I celebrating our 40th anniversary at St Paul's Episcopal
Church in Atlanta.
Catch a glimpse of Vincent Henderson in the background.

Attorney Johnnie Cochran and his wife Dale (right to left), Secretary Alexis Herman, Fred Carter, Leteria, and Joyce Carter.

Me and race car driver, Bill Lester.

Me, Supremes member Mary Wilson, Leteria and other guests.

Garry Bridgemon (far left), William Cooper (middle), actress Gabrielle Union, Bernard Porsche (far right) at Morehouse School of Medicine.

Morehouse School of Medicine leadership team with Dr. Louis Sullivan,
Founding President of Morehouse School of Medicine.

With actress Dawn Lewis and her mother at our annual Christmas party.

Me, singer Patti LaBelle and Leteria.

Henry Kelly (left), Marcel Henry (center), and actress Sheryl Lee Ralph.

Leteria and me celebrating our anniversary in Paris.

My godparents—Ernie and Carolyn Gibson and me.

Me and Hank Aaron.

Clarence Lott (left), Monica Kaufman, Leteria, and Vivian Malone Jones
in Mobile, Alabama for a reception during Mardi Gras.

Me and Leteria with Secretary Alexis Herman at one of our holiday parties.

My youngest daughter Lailee, with Maya Angelou and Leteria.

Julian Bond and me.

Debbie Allen, Coretta Scott King, and me at an MLK Day celebration.

My mentor, Dr. Gaines Thompson.

Soledad O'Brien and me at Morehouse School of Medicine fundraiser.

Our special guests at 100 Black Men's Le Cabaret—Valerie Simpson,
Nick Ashford, and Gladys Knight.

Dr. David Satcher—former President of Morehouse School
of Medicine and 16th US Surgeon General.

With Ms. Coretta Scott King, greeting guests in attendance at an MLK event.

At the Super Bowl with our dearest friend—Vincent Henderson.

Me, celebrating my 65th birthday at the Ritz Carlton Hotel in Atlanta

Mardi Gras, 1997. I was the Grand Marshall.

Judge Elaine Carlisle (far left), Christine King Farris and her son Isaac Farris.

Me and Leteria greeting Maya Angelou.

My in-laws Melvin Seals (left), Edna Seals (mother in-law),
Joyce Stephens, Kermit Seals.

My aunts and mom—Maggie Singleton (left), Catherine
Washington (middle), and my mom Mabel Williams.

Holiday gathering at the Ritz Carlton—my mom Mabel Williams
(seated left), my aunt Catherine Washington, my mother in-law Edna
Seals, Judge Glenda Hatchett and her mother Clemmie Hatchett,
my sister and brother-in-law George and Joyce Stephens.

Secretary of State Colin Powel and me.

Ambassador Andrew Young and me.

Bruce Jones (left), our cousin Carlos Harbert, GA Gov Frank Harris,
and John Grant.

Morris Day of the music group—The Time and US Congressman
David Scott.

Mayor Andrew Young and me.

Congressman John Lewis and me.

Our group meeting Bishop Desmond Tutu during my trip
to South Africa.

Me holding a baby lion on my visit to South Africa.

US President Bill Clinton and me.

My 80th birthday celebration in Sarasota with my friends —Dennis Thompson (left to right), Ron Johnson, John Maupin, and Ralph Hughes.

My 80th birthday celebration in Sarasota with my friends. It was a surprise. (Left to Right) Irene Johnson, Nancy Boxhill, Leteria, Lailee, Lybra and Eileen Maupin.

Me and Leteria at her 65th birthday celebration,
Atlanta Intercontinental Hotel.

Me and Hill Harper.

U. S. Senator Rev. Dr. Raphael Warnock and me.

Just me.

CHAPTER SEVEN

THE BEDROCK OF COMMUNITY

"The greatness of a community is most accurately measured by the compassionate actions of its members"

—Coretta Scott King

Creating A Community of Achievement

There is power in numbers, and in Atlanta the energy around transformation and purpose was kinetic because there were so many heavy hitters for change in the city. I talked about some of the people I met in the last chapter. The significant thing about this group was that so many of the people involved in propelling change had a strong spiritual base. We all bore witness as to how God was at work in our lives because we knew we could not have done so many great deeds on our own. The momentum of everyone working together in harmony was so powerful that even the struggles were often mighty, the efforts 100 percent, and our success were many.

Sometimes though a single flame is enough to light a whole room. That torch for Atlanta's Black community was lit by the first Black Mayor of the city, and of any city in the South, Maynard Jackson. Maynard, a lawyer by profession, was a democratic political heavyweight. He was directly responsible for increasing minority business participation in the city and for improving the airport to the point that Atlanta became an international hub. After two terms as Mayor, he passed the charge to the very competent Andrew Young, who in 1994, became the 55th Mayor of Atlanta. Andrew followed in the footsteps of Jackson and continued Atlanta's massive transformation, which was favorable to Black Americans. Under his leadership Atlanta became an international city.

Andrew Young, Jr., who began his career as a pastor and was a close confidant of MLK, was too, the embodiment of what one man can do. In 1973, he became a member of the U.S. House of Representative representing Georgia's 5th district. He then went on to be an Ambassador to the United Nations under the Carter Administration.

On August 1, 1974, when we moved to Atlanta, Leteria and I were young, excited, and eager to dive into the robust culture the city provided. We had just left white suburbia so it was exciting to be surrounded by Black professionals, and we wanted to be a part of the hopes and aspirations of our people. I wanted to be in on the decision-making processes that made life more tolerable for Black folks.

Jean Childs Young, Andrew Young's wife, had been named Director of Public Relations and was a Reading Specialist, so as educators we were in the same space. As a new educator at Atlanta Metropolitan State College, I was fortunate to have a chance meeting with her. We bonded around that and Atlanta Junior College. Given my deep desire to be of service, and the Youngs' goals to create dynamic and positive change for Atlanta.

My prayers had been answered. I had landed in a place where everything I dreamed of, wished, and hoped for could become possible. Being forthright and speaking up about my desire to be of service, my ardent passion to get involved was further heralded by others. Anyway that I could help carry out the vision of a progressive Atlanta, was something I was glad to explore. The power circle of people I'd become a part of was what I had imagined as a young child. I, at last, was able to fulfill my long held vision to become a person of substance.

The Power of Women of Color

Men were not the only ones spearheading change in Atlanta. Equally effective were the women for change who worked through many organizations.

These powerful women's organizations chose to make a change through active involvement in politics, social and civic groups, Arts and Letters, and Education. Lillian Lewis (John Lewis' wife) and Leteria worked on a number of projects together for the Jack and Jill organization. With two girls in my brood, it was easy for me to offer my support to this organization. In fact, I took pride in it, but it was really my wife's impact on this children's organization that was significant. There were other women groups too, such as The Links and the Greek Sororities. It is easy to reflect on their contributions to the dynamic Atlanta with great respect.

The Public Servant

As a result of my community activities, I truly embraced being a public servant. Fulfilling this role allowed me to see the difference I could make in real time. I got to experience this firsthand, working alongside the heavyweights involved in bringing the Olympics to the city. Ambassador Andrew Young spearheaded the project, and with the support of the African Delegation, the 1996 Summer Olympics were held in Atlanta. It was a priceless experience and because of this, along with its continued robust growth, Atlanta was becoming an international destination and with a new airport to handle the traffic into the city, Atlanta was on fire.

Through the countless relationships that were formed in Atlanta I met people from all over the world, including presidents and ambassadors. When Andrew Young was mayor, it was quite common to have international visitors to the city. People like Nelson Mandela, along with his wife Winnie, came to Atlanta right after he was released from his twenty-seven-year prison sentence. Mandela was hosted by the city of Atlanta and the 100 Black Men of Atlanta, and I was an integral part of that planning committee. Meeting and interfacing with Nelson Mandela was an awesome experience. With one event after the other we built up serious momentum and for those of us on the frontline, there were never a lull in the day or a quiet night because there was so much that had to be done.

The same is true for Sonjia and Walter Young (Andrew Young's brother). Both are actively engaged in the public service arena. They are consistently giving their time, talent, and resources to the community. Sonjia is a retired Event Planner and Educator and Walter a recently retired Dentist. One of the formidable women I met was Glenda Hatchett of the Judge Hatchett Show. Glenda was a major supporter of the 100 Black Men of Atlanta and of our Project Success Program. She became like a sister to Leteria and me and was always available when I needed her support. She and Leteria were charter members of The Dogwood Chapter, The Links, as well as members of the Atlanta Chapter of Jack and Jill. Her mother, Clemmie, who we called Mommy Clemmie, was our advisor and surrogate mother in Atlanta.

An Elevated Game

When I began working at Morehouse School of Medicine in 1991, I was immersed in the community relations that were paramount for the future medical doctors the school trained. As Executive Director and Associate Vice President, my role was designed to be the liaison between Morehouse School of Medicine and the greater Atlanta community. I focused on external affairs and development. How could I help the students transition into the outside world and how could I invite the outside world into the work I did? Those questions led me to bring people like Archbishop Desmond Tutu, Colin Powell, John Lewis, and Congressman David Scott to our campus to talk to our students.

In my position I interfaced across various disciplines important to the community, including politics, education, hospitality, and economic development, and so on. Uniting folks around a common cause gave me leverage that led to positive results toward each of our stated goal being met. The first president of the college that I worked with was Dr. Louis Sullivan, the founding President of Morehouse School of Medicine. He also wore multiple hats as his role extended beyond the college. A physician, educator, and award winning author, he served as the

Secretary of Health and Human Services, under President George W. Bush, who I refer to as Daddy Bush.

Dr. Sullivan's ties in Washington benefited me in Atlanta. I focused on developing a stronger presence within the community through partnerships with colleges, universities, public schools, corporate, hospitality, and within the political arena. I sought out the people with skills in all the areas that informed my work, and had the benefit of Georgia Congressman John Lewis, David Scott, Sanford Bishop Jr., and Hank Thomas as key contacts. Dr. Sanford Bishop Sr, Founding President, and father of Congressman Sanford Bishop SD Bishop State College in Mobile were also a mentor that helped shape my views on life.

Access, relationships, and credibility were needed for my job, and I worked hard to gain the trust of my mentors, friends, and colleagues. I soon became a voice in the relevant conversations being had with mayors and other leaders, and I was able to solicit funds from the state to support our school vision, even though we were a private institution. One of the major reasons for this was that the services Morehouse School of Medicine provided were public, because we trained physicians who would then work in the Georgia communities.

Fundraising was an essential part of my job and I had a natural knack for such things. With a disciplined and organized mind, and a love of conversation and persuasion, I was able to pull things off successfully. But no one ever goes it alone. For example, my strong relationships in the hospitality industry gave us many venue options to host events throughout the years all because of the individuals with decision making authority joining forces with my efforts. I began to believe that I was successful at my job because a lot of people knew who I was, knew what I was doing, and realized that my involvement in a project meant it was likely to be successful. My dream of becoming a person of recognition came to fruition in Atlanta, the city I came to love, and the city that favored me so strongly.

Atlanta met me in mind, body, and spirit, and cemented all my early dreams and aspirations. When I left Atlanta my purpose was fulfilled. That's why it was a shock to so many people when Leteria and I decided to relocate. We looked into locations such as Martha's Vineyard finally settling on Sarasota, Florida.

Leteria and I decided to move to Sarasota, after nearly forty-five years in the city of hope. People thought we were kidding, however, we both recognized it was time for a new pursuit. Sarasota is not entirely Martha's Vineyard, but it gave me enough space, peace, and a place for me to pause.

For me, public service has always been at the heart of what I do. There is a shortage of people who are willing to step into this spotlight. Cultivating the proper connections to be effective on a broader scale takes time. I'd like to think that it may be your time to start doing this, especially if you're a young reader who is trying to find their way in this world.

My Individual Mentoring

I think I can safely say that my life's work has directly and indirectly impacted many people. Much of that effort has come from my work with organizations and my career. But there is something gratifying about holding space for people in your direct path. There is a feeling of fruitfulness as an individual with a God-given directive to help others on their journeys through mentorship when this is accomplished. In that regard, I've been spiritually fed.

This happened when I came into contact with a group of four young men: John Grant, Juan Montier, Henry Kelley, Bruce Jones; and a family member, Carlos Harbert, who had come from Oklahoma and was living with us at the time. These young professional men were, at that point, starting out in their careers. At the time, John Grant was an Airborne Express representative, Juan Montier, an Architect, at the firm Gensler. Henry was a manager at Georgia Power Company, and Bruce Jones, an Independent Insurance Broker. Carlos Harbert was an Investments Manager. Young and single, these gentlemen enjoyed happy hours and single guy things that I really didn't relate to any longer. Because I was protective of my time and I had no idea how serious they may or may not be about becoming leaders of something greater than their jobs at first I resisted their attempts at engaging me.

I was at one of our usual events when John Grant came up to me and said, "I have just been observing you and I've been hearing about you. I would like for you to be my mentor." This kind of request was not uncommon, but it was unusual that people would be really serious about it. So, I said, "I'm so sorry son, but I don't know you." Then I walked away. At yet another event John found me and made the same request. My response was the same, but I liked his persistence. I happened to mention that I was mentoring Carlos, a part of their circle, and I thought that was the end of it.

One night Carlos came home, and I opened the door to let him in. Behind him were all these guys, including John Grant, who said, "I got you now." Yes, he did have my attention now and that was the start of a wonderful ongoing relationship. I began to mentor the group. I began including them in activities by extending invitations for them to have meaningful experiences in the community. When they were ready for it, I introduced them to the 100 Black Men of Atlanta current political campaigns, invited them to social events and other civic organizations. We volunteered at the King Center and helped with the Mayor's Masked Ball. Along the way, we added Michael Pack (the interim CEO of the Hartsfield Jackson International Airport and currently a major consultant in Aviation at airports.) and Darrell Adrian Fitzgerald (an architect at Gensler who heads his own Architecture firm) to this list of young male mentees I had somehow gathered.

At the time John Grant, who was the oldest, was about twenty-eight. Today he is in his sixties. When he turned thirty (the minimum age of the 100), I sponsored him into the organization, and the others followed as they became of age. The rest of the guys are in their late fifties. Our relationships are still strong. We communicate several times a month. There were so many people responsible for my introduction to the city of Atlanta's power brokers, and now I was helping others do the same. It was gratifying to see the next generation stepping up. These young men were committed, truly wanted to listen, and learn, and I was overjoyed to share what I had to offer through mentorship. At times we had to work through the generational gap. Let's face it, people in their twenties and early thirties have a desire to do things the way they want to do them. Ways that they thought were better, and that's not a bad thing…it was just a part of the process. I was not committed to having things done one single way so that didn't bother me. As long as growth and progress were occurring I was happy. And I might say, on either side good lessons were learned as the result of our different approaches. I learned just as much from them as they learned from me. The investment of time and dedication it took to mentor these young men has paid dividends. As I write this, it is with excitement that I recall those interactions, which I count as among my most rewarding work. I am proud of them and humbled that my mentorship has had a positive impact on their lives.

Now in their fifties, sixties, and seventies, married with children and grandchildren, these men have done well for themselves, and it is so exciting to me. They are still involved in their community, and they breathe excellence into everything they do. They are mentors doing their part to be public servants. They make a difference in the lives of young Black men, specifically. They have put in their time, and it shows. John, who is now with ESPN, leads the yearly Celebration Bowl championship in Atlanta between the HBCUs, giving back to the community in immeasurable ways. He was recently selected as one of the top 50 men of influence in football. What an honor. Juan Montier, an executive chef extraordinaire, and his wife run a very high-end and thriving gourmet catering company. Their clients include Tyler Perry, Arthur Blanks, and Valerie Montgomery Rice. Henry Kelley went on to become an executive with Georgia Power. He later pursued his entrepreneurial dream and now has a thriving package delivery business with Amazon. Carlos Harbert is still an Investment Broker and Bruce Jones is deceased. Every chance I get to speak with these men is a moment that I cherish. It was hard during the COVID pandemic, but we still managed to connect via Zoom. I even served as MC, via Zoom, for Michael's 71st birthday.

Earlier in my career, I befriended a young man(Fred Lamar Greene) who was taking one of my psychology classes. He was newly married and sought me out to mentor him and to become his advisor. He and his posse of friends, who were mostly Kappas, were leaders on campus and seeking wise counsel for the next season of their lives. His wife Cookie became a part of the Delta Sigma Theta Sorority. Cookie and Leteria are close and good friends to this day. Fred is a successful entrepreneur in Washington, D. C. and Cookie recently retired as a highly acclaimed educator.

The people you align with determine your path to a certain extent, whether you are mentoring them, or they are friends. When you choose your company wisely, you'll find that they become an intricate part of your life and you become a part of theirs. Friendships add to the quality of life one lives. As someone who understands how to make the most of life and opportunities, I welcome every new friend who adds value to my life and to theirs.

Giving back to people was wonderful, and it affirmed to me the difference that I could make to people just by being accessible to them. I am still intricately involved in mentoring others, such as Sam Carter, a graduate of Xavier University, New Orleans. Sam is an enterprising young man who comes from a very humble beginning, and who has risen to the top of his game as a highly successful businessman and owner of a thriving accounting firm in Atlanta. There is also Lionel Woodyard, a family member from Mobile, Alabama currently living with his wife Sheryl and their family in Atlanta. Lionel is one of the most giving and sensitive people I know. He is consistently offering his time, talent, and resources to help others, especially those in need. He also has a successful Transportation Company.

The ebb and flow of life definitely carries over to mentorship. The joy that comes from seeing another persons' success keeps the flames of hope alive.

TEACHABLE MOMENTS

So much goes into mentorship. Everything must align. Not every good mentor is for everyone who needs guidance. This is where the ability to create meaningful connections comes into play.

A tough question to ask of yourself is this one: how many people do I know that I would trust to mentor me? If you answer "none", you might need to build stronger connections to get to the right group of mentors, or even just a single mentor. If you answered "many" you need to start talking with these people and see the potential.

The teachable moment is to be able to identify when you are being called to mentor someone or to be able to sense when you need mentorship in your own life. After all, it is through these opportunities that your entire life is defined. Mentors don't have to look like you, or even come from your same community. In fact, I can say that I have successfully mentored people who were not Black. Also—mentorship is not transactional. As I mentioned, mentorship is intentional. It takes time and persistence on both parts. The strongest relationships are ones that grow within the mentorship. There has to be trust, and a willingness to learn. Cultivating a growth mindset is key to a healthy relationship with a mentor. What people often misunderstand is that mentoring is two-sided. As a mentor, I have learned more from my mentees. I am forever learning and open to being challenged by new ideas, perspectives, and opportunities.

CHAPTER EIGHT

THE POWER OF WOMEN

*She is clothed in Strength and dignity and she laughs without
fear of the future*

—Proverbs 31:25

Strong, Black Women

With so much of this book focused on Black men in America, I wanted to devote some time to the goodness of Black women and to their contributions. The two women at the top of my very long list of strong, powerful, and influential women are my grandmother and my amazing wife.

It didn't take the Women's movement for me to know and appreciate how strong our Black women are. There were two Black women who became Mayors of Atlanta. Shirley Franklin was one of them. Before taking over the mayorship, she worked in Maynard Jackson's and Andrew Young's administrations. Shirley had children the same age as me.

The archetype, of the Black woman so often bantered about, stems from the days of slavery when women had to see their husbands and children flogged, humiliated, lynched, and jailed, and then had to come home to be the head of their households. Most of these women had to exercise independence, interdependence, and emotional restraint to be solo caregivers for their progeny. I'll be the first to say, and will gladly proclaim for all to hear, that a strong woman is an integral part of a successful family.

As fate would have it I have been surrounded by strong Black women. My grandmother was certainly a powerful woman, as are my wife, Leteria and my daughters Lybra and Lailee. The women I met in Atlanta as Mayors, professionals, wives, and friends, have proven their value beyond a shadow of doubt they are to be reckoned with and have equally left their mark not only on me and those around them, but on many in the very country that never embraced them. I know this list is long but I am going to take a moment because I think it is important that I memorialize the valiant and unsung women of change who have helped all of our successes along. Gloria Hinton Bridges, Beverly Lyle Brooks, Linda Brown, Paulette Lewis, Janice Brazier, Andreda Pruitt, Juliette Smith, Thelma Thrash, Alexis Herman, Maya Angelou, Sonjia Young, Irene Johnson, Shirley Franklin, Billye Aaron, Valerie Montgomery Rice, Denise Whiting Pack, Eilene Maupin, Yvonne Wiltz, Sally Davis, Joyce Carter, Billie Greenwell, Doris Jackson, Carolyn Young, Lillian Smith, Brenda Cole, Monica Pearson, Margie Tuckson, September Gray, Pat Montieth, Sandra Bridgeman, Joyce Moorehead, Tonya Dennis, Constance Taylor, Bessie Isom, Patty Mabra, Lois Sanders Riley. Pamela Hoffman, Nancy Boxill, Linda Brown, Mildred Bell, Marva Watkins, Joyce Stephens, Grace Daniels Abrams, Odette Tyus, Letisha Daniels Jackson, Lorainne Hunter, Ruby Lucas, Renee Gilmore, Vicki Oldham, Vicki Davis, Joyce Bacote, Wonya Lucas, Jessie Watson, Doris Johnson, Wanda Gilbert, Patti West, Cheryl Bayse, Synthia Roberson, Gloria Patterson, Wanda Thomas, Diane Greene, Barbara Yarn, Linda Gulley, Marilyn Thompson, Henriette Antoini Keisha Lance Bottom, Valerie Jackson, Sheila Bruce, Lois Wilkins and of course my incredible daughters. These strong Black women have done so much for our community and are wonderful influences in my life. Again, I must mention my most ardent supporter, mother to my children, my champion, my strength, and the ultimate Black woman for me in my home—my beautiful wife Leteria. All these women directly contributed to the growth of Atlanta. I want to highlight that.

Strong Black women are powerful and their influence significant. Except for a few mentioned, all are as a result of my Atlanta connection. But I was blessed to have three groups of women who have been key and continue to play a significant role in my life. There are my long standing Mobile connections with Alexis Herman, Joyce Ann Carter, and Pauletter Lewis. They are all like sisters to Leteria, and we gather once or twice a year for celebrations.

Gloria Hinton Bridges, Beverly Lyle Brooks, Linda Kay Brown, Margaret Howell, Denise Whiting Pack, Yvonne Wiltz, and Tish Jackson are Leteria's close friends, and I maintain a strong relationship with them as well as with their spouses. We also gather yearly for celebrations. I am privileged to have lived this life with Janice Harris Brazier, Andreda Wilkins Pruitt, Thelma Battle Thrash, Esther Nettles Rauch, and the late Ardenia Wilkins Johnson, who have been friends of mine since high school. Lastly, Pamela Hayling Hoffman, and Sonjia Waller Young, all from Atlanta, have been friends for over forty-five years. Pam and her husband Joseph Hoffman, M.D., currently live in Sarasota. Sonjia and her husband Walter live in Atlanta and are exploring Sarasota part time. The other powerful women I have named are a part of my life as well. Thanks to all of them.

Being a "Girl Dad"

When our second daughter Lailee was born, Leteria took a brief leave of absence from work to focus on raising a toddler and an infant. With the formative years passed, Leteria was eager to get back to work. When that time came, one of my aunts from Mobile, Maggie Singleton, came up to help with the girls. She was with us for a year and made an enormous difference in our lives by allowing us to achieve our personal goals without sacrificing the stability of our young family.

These days, I observe so many men embracing and redefining the concept of being a "girl dad." Perhaps this has been around for years, but more and more men who have daughters are approaching fatherhood as they would any critical relationship—especially with their daughters.

Long gone are the days when women were just expected to hold the relationship with their girls sacred. Circumstances in life and society have certainly shifted that dynamic. I know several men who have had to take full responsibility for their children—due to divorce, death of a spouse, single parent household, or even gay marriage. A more modern approach to parenting—to which Leteria and I have adopted—was that we parented equally. When Leteria decided to go back to work after taking time off to raise Lailee, we both had to contribute. I not only attended ballet recitals, plays, basketball games, violin lessons; but, I was an active parent.

From an early age we aligned both Lybra and Lailee with opportunities to be of service, and to feel connected to their Black heritage. Their young lives were much less chaotic than the life both Leteria and I experienced growing up during the civil rights movement. Still, it was important to us that they were connected to their roots, and to the lessons and teachings we learned from that era, because the work was still not (and is still not) done. Volunteering was the ideal way for us to incorporate a life of service into their lives.

When Hosea Williams asked for community volunteers, we learned to answer that call. Hosea Williams was in the inner circles of MLK's group, and was himself an ordained minister, businessman, scientist, philanthropist, and politician. At Thanksgiving, Hosea Williams, Feed the Hungry, was a major program to help alleviate hunger for local families in need. The program would feed people at Atlanta Stadium during the Thanksgiving and Christmas seasons. The program was also dedicated to helping those in need of food year-round. Having Lybra and Lailee with us during these times of service meant that we could open their eyes to areas where they could give and serve and make an impact on someone else's life. Also, during Thanksgiving and Christmas, we adopted a family in need. We continue that tradition today. We provide food, clothing, toys, gift certificates and special gifts to families.

The children also volunteered at The King Center, where Mrs. King's children also served, forming lifelong friends of their own.

These activities in public service were the start of their commitment to social responsibility, and to building a sense of community. Their willingness to be involved day-in-and-day-out, even on days when like many youngsters they would rather have done something else always made me so proud. It was important for us to teach them that giving back is vital.

Leteria and I also focused very intently on our children's education. We wanted them to have a quality learning experience. There were three top prep schools, all very expensive, located in the exclusive Buckhead area of Atlanta. They were also mainly 90% white schools, inhabited by the children of the rich and famous who lived in those communities. We couldn't afford to send Lybra and Lailee to these schools. And, believe it or not, even in progressive Atlanta there was still an innate desire to keep Black kids out of these schools.

One of the schools, the Lovett School, was one that Mrs. King was trying to enroll her kids into. They were denied entry. However, in time Lovett realized they needed to seek out and become a more diverse and inclusive environment. They wanted the reputation of being progressive and open minded, and so they began hiring a diverse faculty who in turn could recruit students of color. Our friend, Pamela Hoffman, was a counselor at Lovett and recommended us to the school leadership. The reputation I'd gained in the community helped us earn that opportunity. In the end, my daughters enrolled at Lovett and were offered a scholarship for their tuition and fees.

Lybra was in third grade at the time, and she quickly started to love the new school. She was recruited first and went on to graduate from there. Yet there were challenges. In order to deal with ensuring that our daughters were treated fairly and received access to the same level of care it did take us getting involved with the school at various times. We'd sometimes have to meet with the Principals or teachers at the school to express our concerns and have a discussion. For example, we had to be vigilant about our daughter's grades and the curriculum at the school. While we were now living in Atlanta in the 1980s, teachers were still placing Black kids in remedial classes—even when their grades were exceptional. At one point, we had to have one of our daughters transferred out of remedial English class to an accelerated one because her grades were stronger than her white counterparts who were in those accelerated classes. Our points were always acknowledged, and to the best they could, Lovett attempted to accommodate them.

We were also a part of a Black parent's group. United, we were able to find ways to overcome some of the barriers mounted by intentionally racist people and believe me there were some. At times we had to respond to pushbacks from those who were simply unaware and needed to be educated and informed. The unity and support in our Black parent's group proved to be beneficial to us all at different times.

The experiences that came from some of these challenges made the girls develop thicker skin and more resilience. It wasn't always pleasant for them either. We didn't want them to be treated poorly or unfairly but we did want them to have the best education possible. This meant that we had to monitor their every action and never take a day for granted. Lybra thrived at first, establishing a delightful connection with her classmates. She was invited to spend weekends at their homes, and some of them lived in mansions. Leteria and I could only imagine how that felt, because we had never experienced anything like that growing up.

But things began to change as she got older. Her friends no longer included her as much in their activities. We never knew the reasons why and can only presume that they became conscious of racism and privilege in America. Lybra adapted very well because she had no shortage of friends. One of the things we did with our children while they were in those white schools was to provide the Black experience for them through organizations like Jack and Jill. A sisterhood for Black women and their children. Jack and Jill played a significant role in my family's life. Its vision was that well rounded Black children had to have a double consciousness, a theory similar to what W. E. B. Du Bois shares in his book, *The Souls of Black Folk*. Du Bois defines double consciousness as the struggle African Americans face to remain true to their Black culture while at the same time adapting themselves to the dominant white society. My hope and indeed my charge was to expose my children to uniquely Black experiences, at the same time showing them how to make their lives work within the constructs of a mostly white society. Jack and Jill founded by Marion Stubbs Thomas in 1938, now boasts 262 chapters nationwide.

It's important to realize how significant a role they played in transforming our communities and in making the world a better place for our children. The activities that took place at Jack and Jill included parties, cultural activities, camps, lectures, visits to college campuses, and really anything that promoted a positive image and connection to our Black culture. It was so important to us to balance the experiences of Black children in a white culture for so much of their days, encouraging them to stand proud in their heritage and celebrate their Blackness as strong survivors of an inequitable society. Lybra still has friends from The Lovett School, which is a good thing. She mirrors my own efforts to maintain long standing relationships with people from different cultures. With our strong family bonds and values as well as our circle of friends, we had prepared them to function in a white majority without losing their Black heritage and culture.

For Lailee, the Lovett School was not as good of a fit. She was more into the performing arts and culture. While they had art programs it was not their main focus. We had to find the right school to fit Lailee's needs, so we charted a different direction for her. Lailee went to an elementary school, which was a feeder to the North Atlanta High School of Performing Arts, a part of the public school system. Lailee also attended Paideia School for middle school and in this environment, she thrived. She loved being on stage and later on in high school, was part of the Performing Arts Touring Company where she performed internationally and domestically. This led to opportunities to travel the world over, on private planes with friends who had access to great capital. Through it all, she always remained down to earth and kind, and was such a joy to everyone.

After graduating from Spelman College Lailee moved to New York, where she landed roles on a few television shows—*One Life to Live* and *Law and Order*. We were glued to the television for those shows. In addition to her acting abilities, Lailee is a classically trained singer. However, artistic talents alone are not all to which she is limited.

Lailee went on to Cornell to study holistic nutrition with a specialization in plant-based nutrition. Not only has Lailee inspired our entire family to change our lifestyles, she has also impacted so many seeking a healthy lifestyle. Lailee is the voice of reason in our family. She always speaks with purpose and intention. When Lailee talks, we listen! Her humble nature and easy-going demeanor makes her one of the most pleasant people to be around.

Lybra is my corporate-focused daughter and I'd say she is more like me, just as Lailee is more like Leteria. Lybra is an executive in HR and Diversity. Politics and Washington D.C. are also of interest to Lybra. She worked for Alexis Herman when she was a campaign co-chair for Bill Clinton's election. She also worked with Alexis when she was Secretary of Labor, and participated in the Democratic National Convention when it was in Chicago. Honestly, Leteria and I thought she would go into politics after school, but she decided that public affairs was her wheelhouse. Lybra left D.C. to get her MA degree from Columbia University, New York. She began her career at big name companies like Morgan Stanley and American Express, before she took the leap of going from New York City to California. She has excelled at her passions every step of the way, just as Lailee is masterful at what she has chosen to do. I couldn't be prouder of my girls or excited about their future. They have their mother's kindness and goodness too, which I absolutely love.

One funny reflection with Lybra was that her picture was featured on NASDAQ's big billboard in Times Square. Did we hear about this from Lybra? No! A friend who happened to be visiting New York City was walking in Times Square. He looked up, and there was Lybra's picture staring back at him. Excited and flustered, he called us. . We were dumbfounded when we heard it, shocked, and excited but clearly out of the loop. On our next call with Lybra we asked, "Well, why didn't you tell us?" "Oh, I forgot." That was her answer. She was so casual, yet it was an important thing. In fact, she got commendations from all over the country. It is easy to be quite proud of my daughters. They are both continuing our legacy and that speaks volumes about their hearts, minds, and determination.

Leteria is remarkably close to them, and so am I. While they have a special bond with Leteria, they have a special bond with me as well. So, my version of a girl dad is that my relationship with my daughters are just as important as they would be with sons—if I had any. I learned about hair, ballet, boys, etc., and availed myself so my daughters feel as comfortable with me as they are with their mother. I intentionally developed a bond with my daughters beyond gender and roles. I remember a time when Leteria was working and I had to show up to be the homeroom mom (ironic that they called it homeroom mom). I was the only father in the room. But it didn't matter because I was there, and I wanted my daughters to know that I was present. I would like to think that I served as a mentor, confidant, friend, and parent to my daughters.

As a father, you always want the best for your children. And for my daughters, I was hoping that they would be married with two children and living in the suburbs by now. And that is not the case. Call me old school, but that was my generation's quick step approach. You go to college, find a partner, get married, have children, and ride the wave until retirement. I quickly learned that in this day and age, it isn't that simple. People and relationships are much harder these days. It could be for myriad reasons, but I'm proud that my daughters have far exceeded my expectations and have made decisions and choices that are aligned with their purpose in life.

I mentioned earlier about the reciprocity of becoming a mentor. Mentorship goes both ways, so I had to learn the ways of this new generation. I realized that Leteria and I have a marriage that is right for us. And that might not be for everyone. I also learned the way that Leteria and I raised our daughters are exactly who they are meant to be, and that is aligned to their purpose. Do I want grandchildren? Yes. But am I even more blessed that my children are thriving and making choices about partners, careers, children, etc., at their own pace? Yes. In fact, I have a number of grandnieces and grandnephews so our Sarasota house is always full.

Don't get me wrong, Leteria is a remarkable mother who has raised two strong daughters who are valuable to us and who do valuable things for others. I would honestly advise young women today to focus on strong relationships with their mothers whenever possible. As retirement neared for me, it was my daughters who encouraged us to make the move to Florida. They showed me that I had done my part to contribute to Atlanta, and that it was time to move on to a new project.

The Collective Three

Through Leteria, Lybra, and Lailee, other women have been able to learn important lessons. One that stands out to me is our goddaughter Tannis. Her mom was Gloria Williamson, one of Leteria's close friends and colleagues at Clark Atlanta University. Gloria passed away from breast cancer years ago, and her daughter Tannis, was in between Lybra's and Lailee's ages. Her father, Clarence Williams, is a personal friend and was responsible for me becoming an Alpha. Leteria took Tannis under her experienced wings and made sure she understood the importance and benefits of a tight bond with a female role-model and ensured that she would experience the joys of having sisters.

Through this, Tannis became like a third daughter. She came with us wherever we went and was a part of our lives. When she got married, Leteria coordinated her wedding, then helped Tannis and her husband Vladimir move overseas for his job. All these wonderful things circle back to the amazing abilities of Leteria. She has impacted so many lives and has been such a difference maker for many young women. She does so quietly and humbly. She even had a lasting impact on some of the babysitters for Lybra and Lailee. Three of them were students at Clark Atlanta University, Sharon Davis, Deborah Grant, and Cynthia Williams. These wonderful young women became like daughters to us and were extended members of our family. Sharon recently retired as a master teacher in the Chicago public schools. Deborah (Debbie) recently married to a minister, is a leading minister in Atlanta and Columbia, South Carolina. Cynthia Williams is an Event and Marketing Consultant in Atlanta, and recently got engaged. They too have been invaluable relationships in our lives.

There is no doubt the women in my life have blessed me. There is nothing so comforting than receiving their light when you have challenges to face. People helping people is what it is all about, and Leteria, Lybra, and Lailee demonstrate this in profound and beautiful ways.

There were other young women who we invited into our home who displayed the character of women of substance. There is no shortage of women who I could point to that have not empowered their communities and family.

TEACHABLE MOMENTS

Individual differences can be a good thing. There are times when we may try to mold someone into our image as we try to help them. It doesn't take long to recognize that this seldom works, because you need to accept people for who they are, not for who you want them to be.

Magic happens when you take steps to help another person realize their dreams, which makes them unique and different from everybody else. In my case, I had to do this with our daughters, who each had different personalities and goals they pursued based on their uniqueness.

All this leads to the question: How can I elevate someone to be their best unique self? The steps are simpler than you may realize but can feel tough to do. First, you have to meet them where they are, in the process of helping them realize who they are. Know that God created them for a particular reason and for a purpose. Allow people to see that.

Sometimes as parents we try to turn our children into carbon copies of ourselves. We want them to behave a certain way, go into a particular profession, follow in our footsteps, and so on. When we realize that these hopes and dreams of ours are unlikely to happen, things can become problematic for us, and conflicts can occur. But if you have learned who you are and what you want to be, why can't your child discover for themselves who they are and what they are meant to be? I know my comfort levels, strengths, and weaknesses. It is not my place to begrudge others the same opportunity—that is not my decision to make. So not trying to help your children because they won't succumb to your dreams will not help them grow into their best selves. So, embrace their talents and step up to your role as an open minded parent.

Next ask yourself what can you do to expose your children to people who have their interest and who are open to giving them an opportunity to be exposed to their passion and maybe even thrive? Who do you know in the many organizations you belong to such as the 100 Black Men of America as well as Jack and Jill who would be great mentors? People who are content with their work and life are most likely to offer a hand up to someone in need, who too, could pass it on to the next generation. These are so important. We can share values and traits without cloning ourselves over into the next generation. Maintaining what makes us uniquely designed is a key to a well lived life. You can learn to appreciate someone's personality, background, and history, while showing them a pathway out from what has not served them well. I have yet to meet a person who says that their first choice is to live a life of violence, crime, and drug abuse.

All of us can be the intervention that takes the child out of the toxic environment and directs them toward a brighter one. Mentorship from any level begins with mental acuity and a willingness to embrace differences. If you were taken out of our own environment and put in a cut-throat environment fighting for survival, how would we react? Would you just adjust or would you devise new ways to survive and strive? Would you adopt a new way of thinking about our future?

For example, a child may see athletes and entertainers as their success models. And that is great. But what we must not forget is that what children see is what they will aspire to be. This means that if they see drug addicts and violent thugs in their communities, they will become that. We understand these dynamics in our communities, with organizations such as the 100, so we try to help youth see through a different set of lenses. That's what happened to most of us. And that's what happened to me.

The investment of men such as Dr. Gaines Thompson, as well as the deacons and ministers, trusted friends, and family, helped me see how much more I could become. The good doctor allowed me to see a different lifestyle and helped me to realize that I could achieve it. That is a critical point when you work with young people—can they really see a vision? Is it strong enough not to be stripped away when they return to their community where poor choices have been made and crime runs rampant?

This is why the intervention to help people must be hands-on. It has to be involved and engaged, so that folks can see, touch, and feel the vision. And you have to adopt the families as well. If the parents don't buy into the vision, it is another hurdle that you have to deal with, because even parents who are not good role models for their children have influence.

We need people to be involved in our communities to keep our culture, define our legacy, and show our value to the world. None of this can happen on its own. We all have to participate in this foundational work to have any chance at success.

CHAPTER NINE

BEING BLACK IN AMERICA: THEN AND NOW

"The way to right wrongs is to turn the light of truth upon them."

—Ida B. Wells-Barnett

The Civil Rights Movement righted a lot of wrongs for Black folk in America—of this there is no doubt. But we still have very steep mountains to climb to be fully integrated into the country's DNA. To finally realize true equality, institutional racism, entwined in the operating system of America for people of color must be dismantled. This will require a Herculean effort on the part of every American. My life in general has been a good life but I am still forced to face the reality of systemic racism, from childhood to the present day. Despite these setback, I am one man with a voice who has spent my life fighting for change. Racism, however, is so enmeshed in our institutions that 158 years after the abolition of slavery I still feel vulnerable because of my race. I still fear being attacked. I am still denied certain inalienable rights, and I still experience rejection. If we look at what is happening within civil rights and human rights today, it certainly is far from acceptable but it's moving closer and closer to a finish line.

Throughout my life, I have railed against the lack of equality and decency Black folks are forced to face in America because I would like to believe every word of our Constitution despite the challenging past.

I will continue to fight too, until I equally believe every word of the American Anthem, "for the land of the free and the home of the brave." At the end of the day, I am American, and a patriot looking to build bridges that can carry all Americans across to a true promised land of life liberty and the pursuit of true happiness.

The gap between the gains of the civil rights movement and true colorblind acceptance for all is the next hurdle we face as a people. I can stand on the progress made during the civil rights movement but we have never come close to true color blindness in this country. What will this take? And how do we ensure that we are moving in the right direction?

I believe Ambassador Andrew Young's theory that the next level of parity for Black folks will come with moving from Civil Rights to Silver Rights. Financial prowess is the language of American democracy and the Black community has that, spending roughly 1.3 trillion dollars each year. Surely we can muster up the unity and solidarity to overturn the tables that need to be overturned. We must first mentally overcome the notion of Black inferiority even in our own minds and in our own communities. When Dr. Pamela Jolly wrote *The NarrowRoad*, she positioned Black financial capital in a historical context, pointing out that, "We were the only people in America who were capital on America's balance sheet before we made capital." The blood, sweat, and tears of our forebears built and buttressed the American economy. Do we not therefore have a right to claim our piece of the American dream? As Black folks, this alone should make us switch the script in our heads from one of inferiority to one of ultimate triumphant survivors who were able to build a world no one before us could. To see this century's old baggage finally resolved will be a blessing. Almost certainly, our economic prowess is what will tip the scales for us, because in this country money is the metric by which success is measured. As we move further towards our goals we will certainly experience pushbacks. You can count on that. But as a people, we have always had pushbacks, and we have persevered to this point. Now, there is no turning back. We can also count on that.

139

Voting Rights

Once upon a time Blacks were given the right to vote by law, to the chagrin of many. Those dissenters found a host of creative ways to stifle those rights. After slavery ended in 1865, and the Black man was theoretically a free man, the process around voting was changed to disenfranchise ex-slaves. Arbitrary literacy tests and poll taxes were instituted so that only people who could read and write or own property could vote. And these literacy tests were beyond ridiculous. Count the number of bubbles in a bar of soap! Determine the number of beans in a jar by eyeballing it! Memorize something and do it well. Solve an advanced equation despite only having a third-grade education, which in many cases, such as my grandfather, was the case. Many Blacks were disqualified at the polls for all these reasons. All these small and pointless tests left our fate up to chance and our rights often ignored. This deterrent to Black folks, intended by the majority when those parameters around voting were put in place did not stop us.

One hundred years after slavery ended, the Voting Rights Acts of 1965 was instituted. The Act made it unlawful to use these tactics, and as a result, a quarter million Black voters registered to vote. This did not sit well with the white society, and they employed new ways of deterring the Black vote; intimidation and the harassment of our people at the polls are common even today.

Today voting remains one of the most glaringly obvious examples of how hard America pushes back against its Black citizens. The constant moving of the goal post is not random but are nothing less than calculated measures to discourage the Black vote. Let me contextualize this and connect the dots in ways you may not have done. The modern day prison complex is yet another tactic used to curb Black voters. Citizens with prison records cannot vote. It should come as no surprise, then, that American prisons are filled with people of color. African Americans make up 13% of the US population, but 38% of prison inmates are Black. Other obstacles to the Black vote center around unfavorable zoning practices, unscrupulous politicians, partisan election administrators, voter ID requirements, voter roll purge, closing poll offices in ethnic neighborhoods, requiring citizens to travel outside their neighborhood to vote, stipulations against early voting, or against eating or drinking while in line to vote. God forbid you are diabetic! Many Black voters stand in line for three or four hours, only to be told at the ballot box that they cannot cast their vote, for one reason or another.

The only way to overcome these barriers and restrictions is to be determined to vote no matter what. Voting is imperative. It protects your rights. When you do not vote, you give away your power to those who could care less how you prosper. It is up to you, and you alone, to ensure that your voting rights are upheld.

Law Enforcement

As a child I was often stopped by the police for no reason other than being Black. There were times when people in our neighborhood were afraid to leave their homes because of this. It just wasn't safe, and the risk was too high.

My friend Hank Aaron shared a story with me. There were no youth baseball leagues available for him when he was growing up, so he and his friends would play in the street during the day. But as night drew near their parents would call out for them to come inside, because of fear for their safety. This was true for us too in Chickasaw Terrace. Sometimes you did not even need to be outside to be unsafe. At times we would have to take cover under our beds because the KKK was coming to the neighborhood. These sheeted men were always there for the destruction of something or someone, and their stray or random bullets put everyone at risk. The irony was that the KKK was full of law enforcement men. How could the Black community depend on and trust our local police officers who never showed up to stop the KKK, most likely because they themselves were KKK members.

Parents and grandparents in Chickasaw tried their best to protect us from the random bullets fired into neighbor's houses. Black males who were part of the Civil Rights Movement posed more of a threat than Black females, but everyone was ultimately vulnerable to these attacks. The assailants didn't care who they killed. They believed in white Supremacy over every Black man, woman, or child. Our parents would sadly have to drill us on. "Go hide under the bed where stray bullets cannot reach you. Don't walk at night by yourself in the street. Travel in groups."

We were super cautious when there were demonstrations or marches. Even though they were peaceful, there was always the possibility of being shot at, or of some retribution to your family after the fact. It was a most unsettling life.

I was personally never shot at in Chickasaw, thankfully. But like everyone in my community, I was always surrounded by the imminent threat simply because we tried to live as American citizens with civil, human, and God-given dignity and rights.

Things are not much different today. Still protected by the badge, many police officers instinctively treat people of color differently than they do white citizens. They still kill us for no good reason and the level of brutality against our race has shown that these racist practices still exist. The massive numbers of Black murders at the hands of the police, including Eric Gardner and George Floyd, shows how far we still have to go. The spontaneous protests that erupted across the United States and across the world when these men were killed is the beginning of the solution—to shine a spotlight on this ongoing problem, which we hope will begin a process of policies, debate, education, and conversations that help to tighten the reins on policies that must eventually lead to eradication of unconscious bias.

Neighborhoods

America ghettoized Black neighborhoods. The word 'ghetto' was not originally ascribed to urban Black neighborhoods, but rather to Jewish enclaves created by Nazi Germany. The idea of a ghetto is to have people of the same ethnic group in an area where they can be controlled.

Modern day ghettos are described as urban areas with high poverty and crime. For Blacks, these ghettos were created by the unfair housing practice of redlining. In 1933, when the New Deal was created to combat the Great Depression that followed the first World War, this federal sponsored housing policy heightened and worsened conditions in minority inner-city neighborhoods. Mortgage lenders would redraw neighborhood lines, creating forced racial segregation, designating these areas redline districts and denying them access to the federal capital. Redistricting created new neighborhoods such as Watts in LA, Cabrini Green in Chicago, and Soundview in the Bronx in New York City. These geographic zones full of Black people allowed for more precise warfare to be waged. This occurred in the 1970s when the Black Panthers clashed violently and often with the police. And again, in the 1980s when street drugs were pumped in these neighborhoods to thoroughly destabilize the communities with addiction, violence, and other such problems. During this period, our communities reached the heights of unrest.

I recently shared some of this history with a friend and neighbor in Sarasota. He has never known this world through the lens I and many Black people experienced. He was appalled by what I shared, especially when I pointed out that these things happen to us all the time. I gave him a few examples: the arrest of Harvard Professor Henry Louis Gates, Jr., as he tried to get into his home; Christian Cooper, a Black male who was accosted by the police in 2020 while bird watching in Central Park because a white woman had called 911 on him in fear of her life! Will he ever understand it? Probably not but being aware, he can empathize and become a voice of change.

I currently live in a community that is 75% White, 16% Hispanic, and 15% Black. If I were to go jogging and someone saw me, what would they think? Who would they call? Would I become yet another statistic? These thoughts often cross my mind on my daily walks in the neighborhood. Yet we must carry on and claim our rights as American citizens, through protests, civic and political work, and most importantly, the work we do in our communities to unite around freedom once and for all. The fact that we still endure this state of affairs today is because of the racism that is rooted in the American psyche. It is good to know what the problem is, and even better to move beyond it.

Silver Rights: Reimagining Our Future

The phrase 'Silver Rights' was coined by Andrew Young, but it harkens back to the rallying cry Martin Luther King made against poverty and the need for economic parity for all citizens. In one of his speeches he declared, "There is nothing new about poverty. What is new, however, is that we have the resources to get rid of it." This could very well have alarmed America's wealthy and powerful and may have led to his assassination. Because MLK was braided into the American Dream and had a strong hold over the promise for Black People, this was in their eyes a dangerous move. Were he to galvanize the very people who had endured to build the world's economy, what would that mean for America's wealthy and powerful who had directly benefited from the very people they tried so hard to oppress. Was it because they didn't want them to appreciate their greatness? Carrying the message of Silver Rights further through entrepreneurship and financial literacy is John Hope Bryant of Operation Hope. Hope contends we are in the third reconstruction period, which is the era he believes that a visionary President can do for Silver Rights what Lyndon Johnson did for Civil Rights.

For Hope, 'Silver Rights' involves "re-imagining our future, re-framing our success, and seeing opportunity even in the midst of adversity, and never, ever giving up. Ever." A few Black billionaires, both women and men exist in America today, in fields ranging from business to entertainment. They have achieved financial success by the sheer will of their determination. But even bigger than that, as I mentioned before, Black folks are sitting on 1.3 trillion dollars of power. What would it look like if we united around the single cause of economic freedom? Maybe politics and policy have gone as far as they can in the struggle…so how could we, on our own, become involved in our freedom and change the trajectory of our future by uniting our financial power. I truly believe economic parity is pivotal to our future. I also appreciate the difficulty we will face as we move in this direction.

Modern Day Challenges

When we allow others to define who we are and what our priorities are, we get into trouble. That holds true across every aspect of our lives. Our best life is not lived by following others but by defining for ourselves where that best life lies. This has to become true for us over the deep knee-jerk psychological conditioning that has suppressed our potential throughout our history in this country. This hurdle will require undauntable courage, irretractable values, clear direction, massive objectives, unity, and the utmost confidence. We'll need the patience of Job to deal with the pushbacks. But there is an awakening happening in America on all sides of the color spectrum. For me, this glimmer of hope has been worth the struggle for change I have endured.

I am in awe of the young people I meet today who are fighting for justice on all fronts. When I was young, I was shielded from this discrimination and racism much of the time by my grandparents and by the other adults in my community. Today's youth have none of the benefits of growing up during the civil rights movement, and many have no one to protect them or their minds from the physical, emotional, mental, and spiritual assaults they are subject to today. I am not sure who I would have become if, like a lot of them, I had grown up in a fractured family, fractured community, and a political system masquerading as a democracy. In my time we at least knew the enemy, and we were very clear that we did not have the benefits of a true democracy. Now the covert agitators of my past have taken off their hooded robes, and they sit in positions of the highest power. They speak with authority and with honeyed words, and it is almost impossible for young folks to discern the traps that have been laid out for them. The context is different, but the solution is the same. As parents, family, mentors, and even friends, we can prepare today's youth to deal with their harsh reality. How can we prepare and support them as they face their circumstances? We must unite across civic, social, spiritual, psychological, and financial goals. We must remind them of their dark but triumphant history, and we must love them because they are ours.

Solutions for creating permanent change and unity are infinitely harder in today's world and quite different from back when I was young. There is less of a sense of community today, less of a safety net, and as a result more individual desperation. And while it was wrong that it took segregation to have afforded us a better sense of Black identity, I might argue that some things worked in our favor. Integration gave rise to a whole new set of issues and that is why I cannot stress enough that just because we have access, doesn't mean we have equal rights. When people are forced to act out of fear and self-preservation they are not as bold as they could be. Every parent wants to put their children in the safest environment possible and give them a fair and inclusive playing field in which to operate. My wife Leteria and I had the means to do this, to some extent, for our daughters around their education and other opportunities possible, and we gave them those gifts. However, racism still impacted them not just as an undercurrent but sometimes overtly.

There were times when everything was just a bit harder for my children than for their white counterparts. That was why we double down on making sure they had strength of character, absolute confidence, and a loving home.

Family

There are few obstacles more challenging to our youth than that of dysfunctional family systems. Without nurture, guidance, and good solid parenting, problems ensue for the child. There are just so many environmental factors working against families today: poor neighborhoods, single parent households, low wages, poor education, low skills, unsuccessful schools, a lack of outside help, or the absence of mentoring. These things create the context for dysfunctional family systems to exist. If you live in poverty, for example, you worry more about the daily activities of merely existing and paying your bills, than about anything else. There is only so much bandwidth available to us. This is why it is so important for people struggling in poverty to see that there is hope. They need it, just as we all do. Today, more youth than ever before feel that they can't escape their impoverished situations.

Here is my message for the youth. Start the journey to your destiny by facing your fears in a healthy way. You don't have to become a statistic. Robbing, shooting, and looting are not the only means of survival. When you choose those options, you are on your way to becoming the next statistic in the war against our community: you can be killed or put in jail, for example. Incarceration rates in the African American community, especially in poor neighborhoods, have been consistently high, and tells us that we are losing the war.

We also lead statistics in the health crisis. This includes diseases such as high blood pressure, diabetes, and also mental health. African Americans commit suicide at a higher rate than other demographics. Wealthy Black people are not immune. Actually, it could be argued that wealthy Black folks may be more susceptible. Recently, the sons of actor Regina King and business woman Debra Lee committed suicide. These were kids from affluent families who seemed to have every opportunity open for them. Yet something was missing that made their lives dire enough for them to want to die.

People are not always able to cope and to deal with this system by themselves. We need to reclaim the creed of loving our neighbor as ourselves because it still very much takes a village to raise a child. Let's take a leaf from the pages of the Jewish and Asian communities. Let us raise the bar on love and expectations; let's erect barriers to keep destruction out of our communities; Let's advance ourselves to the point of financial parity. Our solutions lie in these three areas.

TEACHABLE MOMENTS

What can you take away from all that I've shared? It is to serve your community with your gifts and passion, because by doing so you will strengthen your community to the point that it is able to serve you. My passion began with education, from my elementary foundation, through high school, and beyond.

What happened to me after high school became the core of all I was able to do, and the ticket to something more in my life. It was how I found a way out of no way by passing the torch of hope to others by becoming a teacher myself.

Teaching gave me a way to see firsthand the impact of my words, and to delight in how I could effect, affect, inspire, and open pathways to success for my students. This was particularly important when I became a college professor.

I wasn't that much older than the people in my college class. I'd graduated high school and college younger than most. But as I embarked on this career journey, I began to learn more about the exciting things that these students were capable of, and the visions they were starting to pursue. And I was in a position to be able to influence the direction of their dreams. This was what I had been training for my entire life without even realizing it—the opportunity to be part of something greater than the individual.

When you find your inspiration and passion, the steps you need to take will be more clearly defined. You will find that your knowledge transcends your fear. This is when the best changes happen.

CHAPTER TEN

TRAVELING THE WORLD

*"We must take adventures in order to know
where we truly belong."*

—Unknown

World travel is an essential part of education. If you never leave America, you will know nothing but the American way of life. Beyond our shores is a beautiful world that can inform, open your eyes, and give you a new perspective. As an African American, there may be nothing more fulfilling than taking a trip to Africa. The fifty-four countries that make up the continent are filled with brilliance and are run by outstanding Black folks in every sphere of life—politicians, doctors, lawyers, architects. These proud geniuses sit on a goldmine of resources. With a rising population median age of nineteen, Africa is poised to become a continent to reckon with. No wonder the world is flocking to Africa as the next frontier, including America as President Joseph Biden stated, "All eyes are on Africa." Seeing an entire country of Black folks operating at the highest level can engender profound changes within the souls of African American who have always felt like a minority.

For me it was an incredibly liberating experience to be in Africa. This was a beautiful place which accepted me fully as a human being, even as my own country limited my rights, opportunities, and my very existence.

Throughout the earliest and formative years, I had never envisioned being able to enjoy worldwide experiences. Growing up in Mobile, my perspective, like many others, was that if we had challenges thriving in our own country, we wouldn't stand a chance in another one. This led me to sticking to local experiences for a long while. Imagine my delight when I learned that although I wasn't always fully accepted as an American citizen with all of its rights under the Constitution, I found a beautiful and inviting world abroad. Not always perfect but delightful perhaps, it may have something to do with how much older and wiser these countries are on topics such as race compared to the United States. But to be fair, many are homogeneous countries that didn't have to grapple with culture and race differences.

When I embarked on a journey to explore the world, I was not disappointed. I found that outside of America, rich and rewarding experiences were available. I could benefit from immersing myself in the world stage at some level, and it was an opportunity available to all who could afford it. My first trip abroad was to Paris, France. I might point out that choosing to go to Paris, and to Europe in general was probably because of subliminal conditioning. Growing up I read and saw movies about romantic Paris, its culture, and its people. Many African Americans from the Harlem Renaissance who relocated for artistic freedom chose Paris as a destination. So, stories of Josephine Baker and James Baldwin in Paris were always a part of the Black cannon. Less known was Alexander Dumas, (père) a Black French novelist and playwright who rose to prominence for his seminal works, *The Count of Monte Cristo*, and *The Three Musketeers*. Leteria and I had wanted to go to Paris years before we were married, so we were thrilled when an opportunity arose to travel there. It was a wonderful experience. I feel fortunate to have had these experiences when so many of my friends could not or chose not to for one reason or another.

After our trip to Paris, we were bitten by the travel bug which led to many more excursions. I was not in the military, nor did I have work obligations abroad, so our travel was purely designed to seek out different cultural experiences, and to breathe new life into our perspectives. Since that first trip, Leteria and I have traveled extensively. We have taken several Mediterranean cruises, which we have thoroughly enjoyed. The beauty of this kind of travel is that we get to see multiple places on a single trip. We fell in love with Barcelona, Spain. But visiting Italy was one of my favorite traveling experiences partly because the maturity and beauty of this ancient culture was evident. We went to Rome—with its laid back vibe, Florence—with its wine country and gastronomic feel, and Venice of course—for the romantic at heart. Unmatched, however, was our visit to the scenic beauty that is Lake Como. Located in Northern Italy, and boasting a backdrop of the Alps, Lake Como is for luxury. We were one of nine couples invited by our close friend Sandra Bridgeman, to celebrate her husband Garry's 60th birthday. Housed in a 10 bedroom suite villa and looked after by all the amenities (cleaning services, boat service, chefs, drivers) it was an experience we will never forget. The robust and magnificent history of these Mediterranean countries created priceless experiences and memories for me which will forever be seared in my heart.

Our entire family has had the opportunity to visit and experience Europe at different times. Lybra and Lailee both spend time abroad. Lybra worked as a consultant in London for six months in the mid-2000s. That gave Leteria and me another opportunity to visit her during her time assignment. Lailee has toured Europe as a part of the performing arts, gracing some of the world's most noted and beautiful stages.

As these experiences unfolded for us, we were able to gain a perspective not only through their beauty, distinct cultures, and memorable architecture, but we had a chance to observe the role racism played in those environments. We found that nations that participated in the Slave Trade, such as France, England, Spain, and Holland, carried undertones of racism but nothing overt like is found in America. It was present on some level, but minimal to us, in comparison to what we were used to. We could fully appreciate why some of our greatest American artists sought the comfort of countries like France. Chester Himes, James Baldwin, Melvin Van Peebles, Josephine Baker, Nina

Simone— were all expatriates in France. They could not find the level of success and freedom commensurate with their talents in America, but they were able to find it in foreign lands.

Overall, throughout Europe and other countries, we came across many Black people operating with authority, and in decision making roles. This was marvelous because it made for such a profound experience. Actually, our third daughter, Tannis, got married and she and her husband, Vladimir, relocated to Luxembourg, one of the world's wealthiest cities, and then later to the Netherlands, which gave them the proximity and opportunity to visit many different countries in Europe over the next decade. When Leteria and I visited them, we saw how they were able to thrive despite being in the minority. There was no apparent racism like what I'd had been exposed to for my entire life, but we realize how racism shows up differently in different parts of the world.

South Africa

Although Europe was enjoyable and informative, there were some life-altering trips that spoke directly to my spirit. One such was a trip I took to South Africa with Ambassador Andrew Young and his wife Carolyn who has been a long standing friend and colleague for over forty years. She is a dedicated community volunteer, former elementary school teacher and a public servant. She is a true partner to Andy and collectively works to serve our communities.

It was my first trip to Africa. South Africa is a majority Black country with a minority white group that had by then been subdued by the fall of Apartheid. I was in awe at the level of respect Andrew commanded. As a former UN Ambassador, he had developed rapport with many, and was pivotal in corralling the vote that led to the hosting of the Olympics in Atlanta in 1996. The South Africans treated him like he was royalty. He was celebrated, feted, and honored by them.

For the first time in my life, I saw Black people providing value and occupying key places at all levels of a country's infrastructure.

Considering South Africa's notorious Apartheid history, I was surprised and impressed at the transformation of the country. The majority Black country that was once ruled by its Dutch minority had become a rainbow nation. Led by the relentless efforts of men like Nelson Mandela, Steven Biko and Desmond Tutu, the fall of Apartheid was celebrated the world over. To see the transformation of a country once steeped in racism rise like a phoenix was the most hopeful inspiration to me of what could be possible for America. I even had the opportunity to meet Desmond Tutu during that trip because he and Andy were good friends. At the time, they were both slated to receive honorary degrees from one of the universities there.

Also inspirational was when we toured Robben Island, which was where Nelson Mandela was imprisoned for twenty-seven years of his life because he fought against apartheid. It was only after that fight was successfully concluded that he was released. That revealed yet another side of a culture of racism, serving as a reminder that the world over, Black natives have had challenges. This was a country in which the wealthiest, smallest percentage of white South Africans had the gall to try to rule over a Black majority nation. In that regard it reminded me of the United States, the difference being that America is still a majority white nation (although debatable that it is rapidly changing to not be). As indefatigable as these men of freedom who fought tirelessly for systemic change were, they paid a steep price. Many lives were lost in the Apartheid struggle and many lives were immortalized as a reminder of the struggle.

My favorite part of South Africa is the capital city of Cape Town. It is a port city, like my childhood home in Mobile, Alabama, and I was drawn to its spectacular beauty and distinct culture. From Cape Town we traveled on the Blue Train to Pretoria the administrative capital of South Africa and the seat of the executive branch of its Government. Naturally, like any novice tourist to the country for the first time I could not resist the opportunity to go on a safari expedition, because I wanted the memorable experience of seeing the animals that exist nowhere else in the world. These are things I will never forget.

China

China was a different type of adventure. Given the hysteria and propaganda during the 40s and 50s about communist subversives, as well as our rocky relationship with Russia, and with Cuba, we had no real idea what to expect on our trip there. Leteria and I literally entered a whole new world when we set foot in the country but to our pleasant surprise it was amazing. Our travels included stops in its two biggest cities, Beijing, and Shanghai. Within this country so many long held views were dispelled. Beijing, the sprawling metropolis, which is the capital of China, surprised us with its laid back attitude, while Shanghai could best be compared to the hustle and bustle of New York City. When I realized I was witnessing a culture that went back three millennia I was truly in awe. The craziest part of this trip was that we didn't see any other Black people. This might have been because as a communist country with an exacting culture, China's borders are not fluid. Though we saw no other Black people, we never had any strange looks. People were friendly, and I felt as if I was viewed more as a person than a representative of a race. It was magnificent. So even with all of the question marks around China's notorious human rights issues, there were no signs of this as we'd been informed about during the trip. We were tourists who wanted to experience a culture and learn. It appeared to us that we were made very welcome to do just that. To us, it was simply magnificent.

This trip took place just two weeks before the start of the Beijing Olympics in 2008. It was inspiring to tour those massive complexes and to see where the world's best athletes would perform, even for a non-athletic type of guy like me. There was no shortage of jaw dropping moments as we took in sites such as the grand Forbidden City.

The International Poverty Crisis

We visited countries where the remnants of slavery and colonialism were still evident. And what is not magnificent is poverty. As many thriving Black communities there are across the world, there are even more that live in dire conditions. You find them in many parts of Africa,

India, and some Caribbean countries. Poverty there impacts every area of people's lives and runs rampant. This takes surviving another day to an entirely different level than my family in Mobile. It was heartbreaking to see and hear about people living in shanties, such as Soweto in South Africa, Daharavi in Mumbai (formerly Bombay), India, Kibera in Nigeria, with conditions so horrible it defies understanding. But closer to home, the island of Haiti was a heart wrenching experience.

We need look no further than Haiti to see the sad reality of poverty. Haiti fought the French and won its independence in 1804. It had to pay reparations to French slave holders and their descendants—the equivalent of between $20 and $30 billion in today's money. This has strangled and crippled the country financially, making it difficult for them to move forward. It is worth noting that Haiti paved the way for many independent countries in the Americas to enjoy freedom (Bolivia, Colombia, Ecuador, and Venezuela). We cannot forget Haiti's contribution to the United States during the battle of Savannah and later the Louisiana Purchase, which according to NPR was responsible for doubling the size of the United States. In fact, our own Frederick Douglass served as the US Ambassador in the late 1880s because of this freedom. As the first Black Republic of the Western Hemisphere, the masses unfortunately are still living under challenging circumstances. Today, Haiti still grapples with geopolitics and other chronic structural forces that need close attention in the international community. Hopefully, someday, Haiti will be "the Pearl of Antilles," that it once was as a gateway to Caribbean bastion.

I—for one—can attest that while pictures of these impoverished communities can be horrendous; those images do not compare to the actual experience. With limited natural resources and tourism as their economic driver, many of these countries fail to thrive in ways others might. Still, these proud people carry themselves with dignity, and while conditions are tough, their situation was quite different from the debilitating mental slavery that still exists in America.
Traveling rounded out what was missing in my education and changed my perspective and attitude even toward my own country. When you

travel the world you will see that all humans are similar and you will realize that we are all connected across cultures. Now, maybe, when we hear of the catastrophes taking place around the world and the human rights atrocities we are more likely to feel inspired to help these foreign countries. The biggest challenge you may face might be how to help other struggling people in meaningful ways when your own besiegement is so dire. To this I would simply say that you may not be able to help everybody, but you can be connected to them and pray for them. Another lesson I learned from my travels is that throughout history, on every continent, homogenous culture or not, some form of oppression has always existed. The thing that warms my heart and revives my faith in the human spirit is that someone invariably always rises up to lead the oppressed to freedom.

Cuba

Cuba, an island in the Caribbean, is a Latin communist country. Its defiance of America, after the *coup d'état* by Fidel Castro, earned it years of sanctions from the U.S. Government. It was once a haven and playground for the rich and famous, evidenced by the dilapidated, once magnificent buildings. But even now there is a grandness to the time-worn country and the music of Havana still remains.

Leteria and I have had the opportunity to travel to Havana, Cuba on two occasions. Once it was just the two of us, on a cruise; and the other was with our extended family by plane. On the cruise we were only able to do short tours because the ship was our base, and we had time restrictions. When we went by plane, we stayed at an exclusive five bedroom villa in the heart of Havana, among the mix of poverty and wealth. This was a luxury vacation as we had all the amenities of the Villa, dined at the best restaurants, visited historical sites including museums and slave trading venues, went horseback riding, purchased art and other gifts known to Cuba and connected to the people. It was amazing and memorable. Havana oolala!!!

Summers at Martha's Vineyard and Hilton Head, South Carolina

There are so many wonderful places to travel in our own country and there are places for Blacks which hold a rich and informative history. Martha's Vineyard and Hilton Head are two such places which are unique and different.

Martha's Vineyard is a beautiful island in Massachusetts located about two hours from Boston. Martha's Vineyard—like the majority of America—was inhabited by Native Americans, and in this case, the Wampanoag People. Over time, the Vineyard was taken over by the English (although allegedly purchased) and it soon became one of the largest whaling industries. As you can imagine, Black people who originally came to the island were enslaved servants and whalers. However, once the tides shifted, Black elites began establishing vacation residencies on Martha's Vineyard and beginning in the 1950s it became trendy for Black doctors, lawyers, and educators to spend their family vacations on the island. The Black history is so profound because decades later, Martha's Vineyard is still a top destination for Black families. Leteria and I started coming to the island with our Atlanta friends in the late 1990s. Martha's Vineyard has played such an important role in my life, that upon retirement, I searched to find that type of peace. In fact, it was a good contender when I was looking for communities where I could retire.

Over the years, Leteria and I always look forward to summering on Martha's Vineyard and/or Hilton Head. These places represented a "utopia" that I longed for—places where I belonged, and where I could see and experience people who share similar values and experiences, all dedicated to the purpose and service. They are places where I could just exhale and relax from the day to day hustle.

When our daughters were young we would travel to Hilton Head, either as a part of our Jack and Jill group or because of my role as Morehouse School of Medicine host when The Georgia State Medical Association held its annual meeting there. It is a place that since the 1800s black families of high net worth and notables and middle class gather to experience the safe haven of a community of freedom. The famous

Inkwell, with the Polar Bears, has been a gathering spot on the island and it holds a rich history and culture for us as African American.

We love everything about the island, the beaches, its rich culture, the hotels and condos, the shops, and restaurants with native cuisines. Lybra, Lailee and their friends really grew up there. Leteria and I look forward to the array of cultural and social events on both the islands i.e., The Speaker Series at Union Chapel, art and culture exhibits, local bookstore signings, visits to Menemsha, the Episcopal Church at Edgartown, the MV Film Festival, delicious restaurants, and the gathering of friends in their homes. Most of all we love the celebration of Black success represented in these enclaves.

One of the good things about traveling with friends and in our home country is that you can still be a part of fun events. On one of our trips to Hilton Head, Leteria attended a Links and Girlfriends events and I had the pleasure of coordinating Receptions and Forums for Morehouse School of Medicine and Clark Atlanta University which featured distinguished guests such as Andrew Young, Alexis Herman, Hank and Billye Aaron, Tom and Joyce Moorehead, Stacey Abrams, Gayle King, Keisha Lance Bottoms, Jim and Ann Gavin, etc. Many of the receptions were held at the homes of fellow community minders, Debbie and Bob Crews, Terri and Lloyd Trotter, Juliette and Walter Pryor, Pattie West, Corbett and Chrystie Price, Aliya and Reggie Brown.

TEACHABLE MOMENTS

As you might have gleaned throughout this book, education is very important to me. One of the best tools for learning outside the classroom is travel. For Black folks, especially when traveling to counties that are predominantly Black, it adds a layer of context, cultural continuity, global community, and history. Because Black history is world history, wherever you go, there is always black history and it should be a source of pride. Venturing outside the American "bubble" to explore world cultures is an eye opening experience that connects us with the rest of the world and allows us to appreciate our full impact on the world.

And there are myriad other reasons why travel in general is beneficial; improved mental health, especially if one struggles with identity, increased creativity from seeing the world in a new light, the broadening of one's horizons by exposure to vastly different cultures, customs, and communications styles. Empathy, compassion and tolerance for differences and for me, most important, are the memories made with the ones I love and have come to love. I included Martha's Vineyard, MA and Hilton Head, SC, as important travel locations right here in our own country because more than being a part of a scene, they are places of solace in our America, which celebrates our history and embraces our future.

CHAPTER ELEVEN

THIS JOURNEY I SHALL CONTINUE

"And in the end, it's not the years in your life that count. It's the life in your years."

—Abraham Lincoln

I am spending this season of my life in Sarasota, Florida, a thriving upper middle class community with an eclectic arts and culture vibe. Leteria and I are two of a handful of Black people in our residential community and at our Episcopal church. I do not have a desire to blend in. I would much rather bring my unique perspective to this world and to my community. Sarasota is a place that fits my soul.

I never imagined life could go by so fast. The truth is when you are doing what you love it never seems like work. After forty-five years of service in the greater Atlanta community, it was time for me to move on to the next season of my life. Atlanta was a city I loved and even helped to grow. How could I leave to go to the unknown? I was following God's will. I felt my work in Atlanta was complete and I knew it was time to leave my place of comfort and convenience and heed His call. I will admit to being reluctant to face the truth. My children had been reared there, I had built a stellar life there, I was well known and established there. This was hard.

I often say that move reminded me of when God told Abraham and Sarah to leave their city, sell all their real estate holdings, leave their wealth and possessions, family, and circle of friends and go to into the unknown. If they did all that, said God, 'He would make them into a great nation.' They settled in the city of Hebron. Bottom line, they obeyed and followed His plan. So did I.

My obedience to my calling has never let me down. After retiring from Morehouse School of Medicine, and before moving to Sarasota, I was asked to join Dr. Ronald Johnson (President of Clark-Atlanta University) and his wife Irene as his Senior Advisor for one year. This gave me the time and space to think. Ron and Irene had been new to Atlanta, having relocated from Houston, Texas. I was going to assist them in gaining access and relationships in the city. Ron, a leading Economist in the country, was assuming the role of the Presidency at the time, and Irene was, and is, an avid patron of the Arts, working in key roles in Houston.

The Draw

Our potential move was just as unexpected for us as it was for our Atlanta friends. We didn't make any grand announcements about what we were doing; however, people gradually found out, and they were all surprised. The more we marinated on the idea of a move, the more I felt my spiritual calling to see what I could do in this new place. I was finally led to choose by the gentle persuasion of our children. Leaving Atlanta was not bad or negative in any way. In fact, I now began looking forward to moving to Sarasota when I realized that it could yet be another part of God's plan for me. He didn't fail me and saw fit to encircle me with good friends. Dr. Ronald Johnson (President of Clark-Atlanta University) and his wife Irene became close friends, who after visiting with us in Sarasota, decided to retire there too.

We were later joined by our friends, Attorney Mack, and Lorraine Hunter, who lived in Atlanta and also had a home in Sarasota. Mack and Lorraine had lived in Sarasota for several years prior to our coming and often talked about how great the city is. Our close friends, Dr. James and Ann Gavin had recently relocated to Orlando, two hours away, so we had a posse of Atlanteans in the Sarasota area. Jim originally from Mobile, is a noted leader in the field of diabetes, and the 3rd President of Morehouse School of Medicine. Ann was actively involved in the city of Atlanta and a major supporter of Morehouse School of Medicine. Dr John and Eilene Maupin, 5th President and First Lady of Morehouse School of Medicine, relocated to Sarasota as well. John was my boss for eight-plus years and played a significant role in encouraging me to pursue fundraising as a focus in my external affairs network. He taught me specific strategies that I still use today in my support of improving the quality of life in underserved communities. That has opened up opportunities for me. Eilene is the event planner and fundraiser extraordinaire. Over the years, we worked on several fundraising initiatives. Eilene and Leteria are members of The Links, Girlfriends, Carrousels. It's been an exciting blessing to have these three former bosses and their spouses here with Leteria and me. It is always great to have their support and counsel.

We recently recruited Dr. Joseph Hoffman (Orthopedic Surgeon) and his wife Pam to Sarasota. We have been close friends with them for over forty-six years. Joe and I are founding members of the 100 Black Men of Atlanta. Pam and I have been engaged in community activities for years. Pam, Leteria and Lorraine were chartered members of Dogwood Chapter, The Links. With us all here and engaged in Sarasota, we have been dubbed "The Atlanta Mafia" and we remain excited about the possibilities of Dr. Walter and Sonjia Young moving here to join us as well.

For the three years prior to our move, Leteria and I had been visiting our long standing friends of forty-five years, Dr. Nancy Boxill, and her husband Dennis Thompson in Sarasota. I must say, they are the ones who encouraged and assisted us in moving to Sarasota. Nancy and her mother, Mrs. Beatrice Posey, were active members of the Church of the Incarnation Episcopal Church in Atlanta. We sat together in the same row at church for years. Over the years, Nancy, Dennis, Leteria and I traveled together, and summered at Martha's Vineyard. It was in the Vineyard that we met Dennis's cousin, Pat West, a permanent resident there with whom we became lifelong friends. Through them, we met others who were snowbirds, living six months in Martha's Vineyard and six months in Sarasota. When Nancy retired as Fulton County, Georgia Commissioner and Dennis from Lockheed and the Atlanta Public Schools, they immediately moved to Sarasota, Florida.

Nancy and Dennis introduced us to their circle of friends, which made our transition easier. One couple we were introduced to by our friends in Dallas/Tyler Texas, Beverly and Willie Brooks, was Dr. Donald and Doris Johnson. Don—a Gastroenterologist, and Doris—a community volunteer, welcomed us to the city, hosted parties of introduction, and served as mentors and good friends. While Don is an active golfer and a lover of music, Doris is a person like me, engaged in the community. She chairs the Board of Directors of the Westcoast Black Theater Troupe, she is President of The Links Chapter, and she is also an active member of Delta Sigma Theatre Sorority and Circle Lets. We will always remember the generosity of Herman and Wanda Gilbert, a perennial couple, whose acts of kindness will always be remembered. They made our transition easy and inclusive. Chet and Jewel Thompson rolled out the welcome mat. They included us in their circle of engagement and Doug and Carolyn Anderson, who we met in Martha's Vineyard and currently live in Sarasota, were also generous and kind by welcoming us to the city.

People call Sarasota paradise, and with good reason. A delightful and thriving city on the Gulf coast of Florida, it is best known as the winter home of the Ringling Brothers Circus. With its prolific Arts and Culture vibe that brings in top shelf Broadway shows and named entertainment figures like Diana Ross, Gladys Knight, Temptations, Four Tops, Cher, Johnny Mathis, Celene Dion, and Kenny Loggins, it feels cosmopolitan. I was delighted to see a tribute to Aretha Franklin done by several of her peers and colleagues in entertainment at the Van Wezel Theater. Another memorable performance was by the world renowned Broadway, television, and movie entertainer, Audra McDonald. The Westcoast Black Theater Troupe, under the leadership of Nate Jacob, is exceptional. Major productions of musicals, plays, celebrity tributes, concerts are thrilling and add to the quality of life in Sarasota. Ballet and opera are pacesetters. The museums offer exhibits that are top rate. For natural beauty there is Shelby Gardens, one of the top gardens in the country. This sounds like an arts and culture promotion for Sarasota, but this city is truly designed for enjoyment, retirement or otherwise.

In addition to all that, Sarasota also has the best beaches in the country, exceptional restaurants, great museums, year-round warm weather, and a superb quality of life. With its serene, lovely beaches and warm weather year round, it is well-known as an enclave for retirees. The only drawbacks I see, are the potential hurricanes and storms that come off the Gulf, and the barrage of tourists from temperate areas who descend on the city during winter months. Ah, and then there can be some hot and humid summers. But none of that was why we moved there. In a nutshell, this is how we ended up there.

Those of us who are seniors and retired come here to just do that. Retire! It's a respite from the business and responsibility of raising a family and building a career. The city is designed for my calling. The water offers me tranquility and peace. The city has developed one of the most unique arts communities. The Arts have always been a draw for Leteria, and the art community appealed to us greatly. It's quite different from Atlanta, but delightful, nevertheless. Being near the water again reminded us of when we were children in Mobile, and it felt like coming home. It took me back to biblical description of being near the water: 'Because of this, one senses relaxation, being at peace and able to meditate'. This was true for us and we are enjoying life—with less bustle and hustle and more personal exploration. We'd forgotten how much the water had attracted us until we returned to it.

The quality of life is amazing and although sports are not my thing, I love living by the golf course near the water. For golfers, it is a haven with beautifully landscape courses everywhere. It resonates well with me and offers me a refreshing backdrop from which to conduct my business in this community. When I retired, I retired from my career, and not from my calling. I may be doing different things now, but I will continue to do what I can to contribute to society until the day I draw my last breath. I am still engaged in my work to improve and impact the quality of life in the community, work with the underserved, and to give back. I'm here living for my purpose, and Sarasota is providing me with yet another opportunity to do that.

The Good Causes Never Die

Wherever you go, there you are. My desire to serve and strengthen my community led me to a new mission in my new environment. My platforms for service were now through arts and culture, as well as mentorship in the Black community which happens to be more represented in Sarasota at 15.6 % than in the nation at 13.6%. Admittedly, it all felt strange at times. I'd moved from a decision-making position in a predominantly Black city, to an area that was very Republican, very conservative, and a majority white community. I had to explore the ways I could gain access to this community. This is a reminder of how important it is to learn to communicate with all people, not just people of your specific race.

My life has grown in ways that I hadn't fully realized it would before our move. As I grew into the fullness of myself I've had the fortitude to look back over my life from my start in Mobile to where I am in Sarasota. For whatever the reason, living in Sarasota has brought an abundance of opportunities for us to extend our services into a new community, as well as to participate in new projects we are passionate about. I have come to see how God's hand has always been directing my life. For this and for all the rich experiences, I am forever grateful. It truly is wonderful.

Aside from enjoying the Sarasota culture, I am also invested in bringing our own Black culture to the area. I invited my dear friend Ambassador Andrew Young to come to Sarasota for a two day celebration of Martin Luther King, Jr. during Black History month at our church, Church of the Redeemer. He was accompanied by world acclaimed vocalist Wintley Phipps. These two inspiring powerhouses, along with other key figures, were in Sarasota for those two days and brought great value and awareness to the Black community: A real chance for engagement and celebration. This is one way my work is being continued to this day.

I am a member of Xi Psi Lambda, Alpha Phi Alpha Fraternity, the Association for the Study of African American Life and History (ASALH), Black Community Working Together (BCWT) and The Church of the Redeemer. Additionally, I am now a member of another invitation only organization called Gamma Xi Boulé—Sigma Pi Phi Fraternity. It's a very prominent, longstanding fraternity of Black professional men. Again, this came about through connections that continue to help me fulfill my mission, as their mission aligns with mine. The goal of the Boulé, like the 100's, is to improve the quality of life in the community and particularly African Americans youth. Currently, I serve as Chair of the Social Action Committee, Vice-Chair for Valentine's at the Ritz Fundraiser, and also sit on the Social Committee for the Boulé. Leteria is an alumni of The Links, The Girlfriends, The Carousels, and the Sophisticates Women Organization here.

Both Alpha Phi Alpha and Gamma Xi Boulé members were asked to work with at-risk males in the Sarasota/Manatee at Booker and Southeast High schools in the hopes of making a lifesaving difference for young students. Many of us get their issues. Though we've been removed from hardships for a long time, we know how debilitating it can be. Facing insurmountable odds, our Black boys need saving. Crime, violence, drugs, sex, and high dropout rates are serious problems that shape their context, and as mentors we have a lot of work to do. As you look at your community, I am certain you can see areas where there is work to do as well. If not you, then who will be a source of help?

I continued my mentoring focus with two Black men in Sarasota— Mark Smith, and Jean Ozit. Mark was introduced by a mutual friend and instantly became a member of our family. He is a little younger than Lybra and Lailee and adjusted well to our family structure. In addition to working at Ringling, he chaired the Board of Directors at Visible Men Academy. Visible Men Academy (VMA) is a charter school for at-risk boys, grades 1-5, in Bradenton. Mark and the CEO, Neil Phillips, asked that I serve as a consultant to the school to build its board and expand its presence in the Sarasota/Bradenton communities. Mark is now Director of Development, at Cornerstone, Inc. Jean comes from a single parent family father environment and possesses excellent academic credentials. We met at Walgreens where he works part-time as a student at State College of Florida. We had many counseling and information sessions and I noted he was somewhat limited in the African American experience. He was not familiar with Historically Black colleges. I recommended that he travel to Atlanta to explore the Atlanta University Center School campuses. He was excited about Morehouse College, sought admission and was accepted. However, because of COVID-19, and the college's restriction, he chose to attend Central Florida State University where he will graduate in May of 2023. He will attend law school in the Fall of 2023.

Bringing Communities Together

I grew up in a time when education was emphasized as the way to improve our plight. I still hold that true for today. Education in the face if insidious racism is the way out of poverty. It doesn't seem to be as much of a focus for families as it once was, at least not in impoverished communities but it is an imperative to reignite the desire for education. Education holds the keys that open so many doors and opportunities.

As a professional Black man and a Christian, I willingly use my life lessons and the influence afforded to help people see and feel how much they were loved, and that what happens in their lives matters. I continue to offer all I can to those in need. I know, from where I stand today, that my entire journey has been uniquely designed for me and I could not be more fulfilled. It may not be your journey but there is a journey designed just for you and as you travel your path I hope you will remember this: You can be revered by kings and queens but if you don't help people in need what have you really done? When we reflect on what we can bring to our respective worlds, the great question to answer is whether we bring community together for the greater good!

Here in Sarasota, Leteria and I belong to The Church of Redeemer, the largest Episcopal church in this area with 2,500 members. In the congregation there might be ten Black members. Possibly less. However, under God's roof there is a home for everyone and a chance to connect and learn about God's word and each other. We may have cultural differences, but as humans, we all have the same desire to live our best life. Obviously, this may mean different things in your culture and based on your philosophy, but we are all here together in the name of God living out our unique and special lives. If our intention is real and genuine we will always find ways to work together, to sit down at the table to talk about our differences but most importantly, to find our commonalities?

We must leave our burdened history in God's hands, because He can do in a minute what we may never be able to do in a lifetime. It could very well be in this church group that we find the kernel of hope, where forgiving begins and spreads to all. I see this so clearly and feel that it is a part of God's work for me to be an instrument in this environment. I am good at playing any role that builds bridges, notwithstanding our brutal history. Limiting myself to the African American community would be like driving on a one way street, when a two way street offers more options for the kind of change needed in America.

It is no easy challenge to keep our legacy and our history at the forefront of American conversation and in trying to find opportunities for us to level the playing field. Like Jackie Robinson, who broke the color barrier in baseball at the urging of his white manager, I believe it will be consensus on both sides that will bring about lasting change. How do we do that? I think we need to embrace all of the differences that exist in America and use our collective power to make unique contributors to advance diversity in our communities.

Giving Back

From what I've experienced, few things can feel as appealing or as satisfying as using the gifts you have to help others to succeed. There will never be anything that can be a substitute for mentorship, leadership, and providing positive examples that help others gain awareness and the courage to act upon their conviction. It is what's lacking in the world today and that has to change. We need to engage Black people in a greater vision of themselves, for uplifting their lives and others. In doing so they may desire to take on this important role of service. The future is reliant on this.

It has been a real joy to see gratitude on the faces of people who have wanted and received guidance from me. I have always stressed in my interactions how important it is to give back in one way or the other. One of these people I mentored who I am most proud of today is the son of my friend Rollie Steele's. Rollie and I went to school together from first grade through high school and were in different social groups. He was a band member, had excellent academics, and was very active on campus. After I got married and moved to Chicago, I taught at the College of DuPage at a time when there was a movement to make the place more diverse. I recruited Rollie to apply, he got the job, and he was magnificent at it. In time, when his son, Rollie Demetrius Steele, (Meechie) indicated that he wanted to become a doctor, I took him under my wing and offered him the same mentorship that had been given to me. Meechie practices medicine in Mobile, Alabama. He is married with two beautiful daughters and after his mother Virginia passed away in 2021, he brought his father Rollie back to Mobile to live with his family. This to me was the ultimate giving back. In addition to Meechie, two of his best friends in Mobile, Alvin Hope and Ricardo Wood (both attorneys) have become a part of my mentoring circle. Both are married with successful spouses and children.

I always advise personal development coaching to help people determine their personal best response to any circumstance. This type of coaching demands that you explore how you view yourself. It is still beneficial to me, even at this time in my life. As I reflect on my life in this book, it's therapeutic to come to terms with how and why I have made some of the choices that I have. This includes mistakes.

We're going to make mistakes. We're going to do that. The important thing is to understand what to do after you have made the mistake. There were days where I could have been very bitter living in Sarasota. My community was too white. My church was not Black enough. All these things could have dragged me down and removed me from the purpose of inspiring others. I am telling you that you can live a beautiful life in any world and surroundings you choose. You have value and purpose wherever you go.

Today, I am the only Black man in two of my three bible groups. The third one has one other Black man. These groups are opportunities to have meaningful spiritual exchanges, dialogues and conversations about brotherly love, and the tenet of all love—to love our neighbor as ourselves. But if you don't know your neighbor, then it's difficult to do that. Community is more important than ever. I've had influences in my life that shaped me just as I have helped shape others too. What shape would someone take if they followed your lead? That is what it all boils down to—following good leads over bad. My deep desire at the end of the day is to see the rise of our Black community once again where values, morals, commitment, and true nurturing becomes the ship that carries us across.

A great representation of legacy not forgotten is the yearly birthday celebration in honor of Dr. Martin Luther King, Jr. It's an enriching, diverse experience. Ministers and leaders from all levels of society and religions are there. In 2022, the first African American Primate of the Episcopal Church, the most Reverend Bishop Michael Curry, Presiding Bishop and Primate of the Episcopal Church, spoke at this ceremony in Washington D.C. Lest we forget we need to celebrate our heroes not erase them from history. Reverend Bishop Michael Curry also presided over another historic moment of racial progress, the marriage of Prince Harry and Megan Markle, representing a massive change to the past for the Royal family. Thirty years before Leteria and I had the distinguished pleasure of hosting him at our home for a brunch, when he came to Atlanta to install Father Rick Brittain as Priest of the Church of the Incarnation.

For the MLK ceremony, Curry talked about what is really needed for a revival of love. This has been a major challenge for us because we currently don't tend to love our neighbors as ourselves because if we did, then we wouldn't be having all of these issues that we're having in this country. No Black person is exempt from intractable racism and scrutiny of our country. As a Black male, you live under the guise of threats, racism, and violence. You're often viewed as the perpetrator, the person out to do something wrong. I take a risk when I decide to go out and take my morning walk in my all-white neighborhood. People's first impression is that I don't belong there. How do I change that perspective? By building up friendships, by taking opportunities to gain understanding, and by starting to have serious conversations.

This is your calling today, at this moment. Start the awkward conversations and let whomever you're talking to come to their own conclusion about you. And be confident that you are a valuable person with something important to offer. My spiritual grounding combined with my immersion in rigorous academics helped with all that. I longed to connect with others and education was the medium in which I conducted this effort. When I went to IU it paid off well, in both knowledge and with the mental liberation that came from finding a way to fit into a world that was dominated by people who didn't look a whole lot like me skin color-wise, though mentally and intellectually, we were on the same or better playing field.

Examining my life at the crossroads of choices, I had become introspective about my unique design. Awareness of my authentic self was the fuel that kept me honed-in on being diligent about attaining my greatest goals, which involved being someone that had an impact beyond my community, a good social and economic status, as well as the opportunity to shake all my neighbors' hands and perhaps call them friends, regardless of the color of their skin. You see, to a young mind being nurtured by education, the pinnacle of success is when you become recognized and accepted for who you are and within the profession you have in every world you inhabit.

Success for me was defined by my ability to connect with the world in meaningful ways, advocating for justice when needed, change when desired, and for anyone to know that if they put in the work and time, they will not be denied their rightful spot at the table, along with the same benefits that others get when they arrive there. That was my life's purpose and for me, it grew into so much more.

Looking Inward

Knowing is a fundamental need for all people who want to understand their greater purpose. Knowing helps you understand where you are during certain stages in your life, how you can evolve, and the lessons to grow with. All of this reverts to the question most people wish to answer before they die: what have I done that has brought purpose and meaning to this world? I didn't always understand that early on but with time to reflect now I do. I am still learning and it's a daily process.

Love has defined my life. Honesty is my fortitude. Community is my desire, and equality is my goal. I shared these experiences and in doing so have also helped others see the challenges I faced, as well as the rewards of effort of truly caring about a community of people. The journey has been the story of my life and its experiences my stage to learn, grow, and help others. As I begin to appreciate God's calling for me to go to Sarasota, to a community the exact opposite of Atlanta, I am cognizant that the work to be done here is bridge building. It is the next part of my journey and I embrace it. It represents all I had envisioned as a child in seeking to be of influence in a world beyond Chickasaw Terrace.

TEACHABLE MOMENTS

There will always be racism and prejudice. It's a condition of the heart to judge, which is where the entire matter can first be resolved. The way to navigate through this is to focus on what will serve you well in life.

Education is key to this. Really, it is. In order to best understand people who are not like you, you need to learn about them. Understand their styles, behaviors, and concerns. Once we'd left Tuskegee for that Chicago suburb, Leteria and I had been thrown into this new white world. It could have been scary, but it became an opportunity to grow into wiser, compassionate, and dedicated people more suited to the tasks we wanted to do. All these experiences have shaped me and I can see exactly how I have evolved and grown to function in these environments.

I grew up knowing God had a plan for my life, just as he has a glorious plan for yours. Admittedly, I didn't always recognize the patterns and growth as they were happening. But I know that there were periods of nurturing and stillness, designated moments in time that allowed me to grow in the ways I needed, so I could be better prepared for service.

Now that I am older, I look back and understand the "why" of my life. I know that what I've gone through was necessary, and I clearly understand how I have arrived where I am today. Once you recognize this same thing in you it becomes your duty to act on it and start to have an impact on others' lives.

CHAPTER TWELVE

PROLOGUE: GOING BACK TO MY ROOTS

"I've learned that people will forget what you said,
people will forget what you did, but people will never forget
how you made them feel."

—Maya Angelou

Since I left Mobile, I have fully inhabited what it means to be a minority. Pushing past the artificial barriers of deterrence has not been easy yet I have never wavered on bringing the community together whenever possible. The way I see it is that everyone can benefit from stronger communities, not just the individuals being elevated. At church, this happens rather seamlessly because the focus is on what's above, first, and how we can bring that to what is around us, second. We are all the same, children of God who can either choose to serve or avoid being of service. I choose to serve.

The same thing is true for Vivian Malone as she walked through those front doors at the University of Alabama. She was threatened, mocked, ignored, and yet found the personal strength and integrity to be a stand-up woman that dealt with that gracefully. Then there are people such as Charlayne Hunter-Gault, who is here in Sarasota. She, along with Hamilton Holmes, integrated the University of Georgia; and the list goes on. These courageous civil rights leaders, whose lives and families' lives were threatened, had to live in fear but they didn't fear because they had faith in God. That fearlessness served a purpose—it had a particular reason—and that was to make the changes we have seen today.

So much effort went into removing those atrocities from the past such as not being able to vote, going into certain restaurants and hotels, or having the kinds of jobs and educational opportunities that others had. Moving past those things back in the sixties took stamina, faith, and determination. Today, we are calling on leaders to address and remove the obstacles that remain in the path of true equality for all. We know we are in the image of God, but we need to resolve how we are in the image of each other here on this earth.

If we only lived for ourselves, if we didn't serve a bigger being or reflect on the sacrifices that our parents and grandparents and great grandparents made in order for us to sit where we are sitting now, it may not matter what life you've lived. You see, a life worth living is one that leaves a legacy, a footprint, a better way forward for our children, grandchildren, great grandchildren, and so on. There is no time to fold up or retire from work. This is why I know that Sarasota, for me, has a different purpose than retiring. And in addition to the opportunity for bridge building, I believe that God has me here to build on the purpose that has defined my entire life…to reach back and bring others forward and that's just what I am doing.

Today, I continue my work in a new location. Same mission, different place. I have worked on a consultant basis with Visible Men Academy, and I did that because these are kids from dire and impoverished situations. 6% are homeless and 92 or 93% live below the poverty level. That is where the greatest need lies, and I was glad to hitch my wagon to that because it has a good purpose—to reach kids at a young age and show them they don't have to accept their impoverished circumstances. I have helped to develop programs for these kids and bring in resources. My daughter Lybra donated a bus to the school because they needed one and did so in honor of her mother's birthday. These things are so beautiful to see.

For a recent birthday, I asked that people not send me gifts but contribute to that school instead. That brought in over $30,000 and it meant the world, to that school and their programs. It's these kinds of things that matter greatly.

We adopted a family during Thanksgiving and Christmas because most of these kids are fatherless. These kids live from paycheck to paycheck and lack even the basic things that get them by in life. This act of love has also given me an opportunity to really know the family's situation. Because if you are adopting the kid and working with them, you also need to work with the family. There is no way around this, especially for a student who is at school from 8:00 am until 3:00 or 4:00 pm, and then they're at home for the rest of the time. Knowing how they spend that time matters.

The family structure and that environment is critical. You also must look at trying to change the thinking level of the families. There is not a universal formula to do that. It takes time and personal attention. You'll need to find ways to help them get jobs and ensure they are receiving the additional support they need from the city or the state, helping to make sure it is done appropriately. Because if the kid is going to survive academically, they're going to have to have that environment at home, in a place where they can continue the learning that they experience at school.

For example, a child can't learn how to read if they don't have lights on at home to read. If they do not have a computer, how can they learn how to use one, which is certainly necessary in today's world? These are examples of what I see as changing the community, having an impact, and bringing people together.

For the sake of propriety and effectiveness too, Black women tend to work closely with Black girls and the men work with the boys. People involved in this work are passionate about it and committed to seeing it through. Fundraising continues to be the one thing that will never go out of style, but people involved in the actual mentorship is what makes all of this magical. There are two parts to the process, so to speak, the individual who work things from a philanthropic perspective and those who are deeply committed to the actual work of connecting with these kids. Both roles are essential, appreciated, and good deeds. What's incredible is that these efforts are not just Black community members alone, but people of all races and backgrounds within the community. Good people exist everywhere and at times it is up to you to ask them to help. You cannot just assume they will volunteer. Learn how to connect them to the importance of your task and your work.

This allows everyone to see what the issues are and where they are. It's more than a big party; it is an opportunity to educate, inform, and inspire action. I am grateful for every person that I have inspired, whether we meet or not. These are people who live out a deep and spiritual calling to be a difference maker in their present world. These are the people that my quote from Pope Francis at the beginning of the book spoke to and is worth repeating. "Rivers do not drink their own water; trees do not eat their own fruit; the sun does not shine on itself and flowers do not spread their fragrance for others is a rule of nature. We are all born to help each other no matter how difficult it is. Life is good when you are happy; but much better when others are happy because of you."

Remember, you don't have to accept life as it is because of your circumstances; you can rise above that. There is a bridge that you can cross that's above the circumstances. Yes, we all have them. We all have challenges, we have low points and high points; however, it matters what you do with it and how you handle it. I look at the heroes in my life like my first hero, my grandfather, and other men of that caliber and the stances they took in life. They sought spiritual grounding and worked to improve equality. It came at great sacrifice, yet it brought our communities together. These unsung heroes are the glue of the family. I hope I have been such a man.

I chose to take a page from the Diana Ross' song, "It's My Turn." I see that it is my turn to give back, to share, to help the least of those, to contribute, and that gives me the happiness that I have sought in my life. You have a tremendous opportunity to do the same thing.

When I return to Prichard, I marvel at how different it is now from the place I grew up. I no longer have close family there. My grandparents' house still stands, but it has different occupants—a Black family with their own sets of challenges to overcome. Do they focus on education? What are their worries? I wonder too, do people have the same influences I had? The ones that dared me to dream big and drew me to a life beyond the walls of my loving home and community. Did these new inhabitants think it important to give wings to those who dream of flying? I have wondered about all these things. Leteria still has family in Prichard, and they live in the same houses they did when we first met. The community has changed dramatically and the physical marks from the crosses that were burnt in the front yard are gone. But the memories live on.

Prichard settles in my memory not because of the pain of the times we lived in, but because of the courage I saw in my community. Though doing the right thing often came at the expense of their safety and security—they never wavered in their fight for the freedom they deserved. My path has been different economically but the ignited fire in my belly to illuminate the world with a message of achievement and goodness is the same.

The church still stands in Prichard, but I doubt that Sundays are still dedicated just to church. I remember the old church ladies, who gave us a little change whenever they had it. Whatever they scraped up meant the world to us and it felt like a million dollars because it came from their hearts. I recall the elders who loved us and prayed earnestly for our well-being. Who was the new Papa who encouraged the children by bartering candy for their good grades? Who are the new Big 9 in the life of a striver to bolster their aspirations and dreams and validate a world beyond Prichard? Where was the village that raised us? I can only hope some of the legacy was handed down in one form or the other. Close knit communities mean people care about each other. That care makes all the difference in the world because there is power in numbers, and in a community with God at the center, nothing is impossible.

African Americans need to look at other ethnic communities that have built barriers against infiltration. Jewish and Chinese communities have erected economic guardrails to ensure that the dollar circulates in their community up to nine times before it leaves. As a result, they have a tax base that gives their community the advantages of better schools, better housing, and better education, all of which translates into upward mobility. The Chinese in particular stress education, and work desperately to get their children in Ivy League schools. Harvard today admits more Asians than any other ethnic group. With the recent reversal of Affirmative Action by the Supreme Court it is yet to be seen how this plays out in communities of color.

We can see the effects of group dynamics and solidarity in Miami where Cuban Americans have built an economic and cultural fortress. Today, you are unlikely to hear English being spoken at the Miami airport. These groups have understood the power of money and how it works. Black communities across America need to become fortresses against annihilation and that is why the work must continue.

In the kind of community I grew up in, if we had a solid economic base, we could have been Miami, Vancouver, or Brooklyn. With 1.3 billion at our disposal, the African American community should be much closer to the Silver Rights equality we desire. That is why organizations such as the 100 Black Men of America drive financial literacy. Once we understand money to be the currency our democracy is built on, we will have unlocked an important part of the puzzle to Black equality in America.

As Black Americans we have significant challenges to face up to. We must rebuild our communities as safe havens for its members; we must continue to seek the best education because that opens doors and puts us in the "rooms where it happens;" and we must unite on every front, psychologically, politically, socially, and economically. The burgeoning Prison Complex must be stripped of the Black population, and second chances must become a part of our story.

I'm a believer in second chances because I was given many second chances. When I faked an illness at Tuskegee to gracefully get out of college, there could have been dire consequences. As a child I liked to rebel and didn't always listen well. Once I took out my Aunt Catherine's car without permission and totaled it. She was a teacher and she worked fifty some miles away. Thinking of how that impacted her, I am still in awe at her response to my delinquency. She didn't lose faith in me. She used the moment to help me to think about the relationship between action and consequences. Imagine too how my life might have been impacted if I had been berated and considered useless for that single act of being a teenager.

Maturity is a process. It is not instantaneous and that is why we must give leeway for the mistakes of the young. To me, this is the core of growth. As a nation we are young and inexperienced. It was only after I visited countries with 5,000 year old histories that I realized time is indeed a significant equalizer. We can and should be open to learning from many cultures around the world how to make our way to becoming a harmonious society.

Since I left Mobile, I have fully inhabited what it means to be a minority. Pushing past the artificial barriers of deterrence has not been easy yet I have never wavered on bringing the community together whenever possible. The way I see it is that everyone can benefit from stronger communities, not just the individuals being elevated. At church, this happens rather seamlessly because the focus is on what's above, first, and how we can bring that to what is around us, second. We are all the same, children of God who can either choose to serve or avoid being of service. I choose to serve.

Is it easy? No.

Is it challenging? Yes.

Given the struggles and the challenges of today's generations, it is so important to have mentors and leaders in the African American communities and organizations who can steer wayward ships back on course. We require new tools and new perspectives, to change these contemporary tides we face. However, I cannot stress enough how important and necessary it is to find these leaders.

I know I cannot save everyone, especially people who don't want to be saved. But throughout my years as a Public Servant, I have seen and have been a part of stories of triumph, and I know that I will continue my work as long as I walk this earth. It is always frustrating to lose a flock but knowing you gave your best effort matters too. You never know who is watching and how your actions may positively change their perspective in the future.

People took a risk on me and that's what I want to do for others. When I see someone who's incredibly talented with the potential to develop certain skills, I can be there to help them make it happen. That's why it's so critical that I, as well as other professional Black men excel so that we can be viewed as role models. We can testify that we have risen past our challenges, and we can prompt them to do the same. So, stay open minded because everyone is going to need a second chance at some point in their lives. Second chances gives hope, and as they say, hope springs eternal.

Reach out and touch someone. As humans our lives are a continuum, and we are all connected. Relationships start with the courage to communicate, to reach out, and to touch someone's heart. Take every opportunity you have to connect, especially with other Black people in the community. Step by step we can begin to rebuild the bedrock for Blacks to succeed…community!

When Leteria and I were first in the Chicago area, we went to an upscale mall called Oak Brook Mall. It was so rare and treasured to see a Black person there, that when we did we actually went up and introduced ourselves. I have done this a million times. It takes this type of courage and directness to build a meaningful social circle.

As I write these words, I am sitting on my deck watching my friends playing a game of golf. It is an activity I coordinated for those of my friends who are lovers of the sport. I don't particularly love golfing but I love having the opportunity to connect others in any way to have meaningful conversations. It's a joy and the least I can do to give back to these amazing friends. These are avid supporters of many causes that matter greatly to me. They are always present at cultural events that bring people together for good deeds. Developing a robust network of people gives me access to the right person for every occasion, whether it is the arts, fundraising, dinner, mentoring, and so on. My contact list is priceless. I have been offered large sums of money for that list. I have often heard it said by successful people that we should "change every-thing necessary but our values." Yes. It always comes back to values. Values are the foundation of a culture, and values shape the individual in that culture. Value is defined as a person's principles and standards of behavior as it pertains to what is important in their lives. What makes them unique and whole? A simple example of this is that I know what my friends value and I try to add value to their lives.

They too know what's important to me so if they are watching a game of football it is rare that I would be there. I won't want to watch it anyway. I value people for who they are, not who I want them to be, and this makes my friendships rich and diverse. We don't all like the same things, but that means there are opportunities to gain experience and grow in various areas. I am non-negotiable about altering my values to fit what is the flavor of the day. Be true to your values and your rudder will direct you to a clear path. And when your path is clear I hope you will celebrate your uniqueness by becoming a force for good. If your calling is to live out loud and that is the life that has been designed for you—heed your calling. A life of service, humbleness, and positivity is the calling I heeded.

As Americans we are already an incredibly diverse nation with so much to offer the world. That is why 163 languages are spoken in America today because it is filled with the hopes and dreams of the world and it is this overlapping of different cultures that has made us a powerhouse. As a country we know that. In order to attain the true promised land that America can be all we have to do now is to accept it fully. Real diversity is an advantage, and it can only be harnessed for our use if each of us, one situation and one person at a time, starting with you, make a change in our perspectives. Imagine with me a coun-try, already a superpower where "One Nation Under God," is a reality.

There can only be one vision. Unstoppable. America, though it may not fully recognize it, has been given a lot and to whom much is given, much is expected.

My life has been a journey, and a magnificent one. A journey designed for me by God. I thank Him for all the rich blessings and the many challenges that have helped me to grow. I've come to realize that I am here for a reason, that is, to be a blessing to others and bring them to Him. He has allowed my light to shine so others can see my good work and to give Him glory and praise. This book shows that. I hope that this will be a message to others to follow His will not yours.

TEACHABLE MOMENTS

For this last teachable moment, it is my greatest wish that you will take the time to see what areas you can make a difference in for someone else. This is a noble undertaking worth pursuing and you can only grow stronger and better for it. Not only does it feel right to do this, but it is the right thing to do.

Knowing this is fundamental for people with a heart for service. Knowing helps you understand where you are during certain stages in your life, how you can evolve, and lessons to grow with. All of this reverts to the question most people wish to answer before they die: what have I done that has brought purpose and meaning to this world? I didn't always understand that early on but with time to reflect now I do. I am still learning and it's a daily process. The journey I traveled has been the story of my life and the experiences afforded were my stage to learn, grow, help others. And all of this defines the teaching moments I've shared in the hopes that you, too, will find your purpose and fulfill your destiny by living out loud, the uniquely designed life that has been intended for you.

ACKNOWLEDGEMENTS

A s I look back on my life's journey, I see that I've been positioned on a path that had been led by spirituality—one with a "divine order." I didn't always recognize that at the moment. The longstanding friendship with Phil and Odette Tyus that began in Mobile , continued when we lived in DuPage County, Bloomfield, Connecticut, Malvern, Pennsylvania and back to Mobile. Phil is no longer with us, Odette is close to us today. Robert "Bobby" Brazier and the Brazier family played such a vital part in my life. He is no longer with us but Janice and I have been like brother and sister since high school. Al Stokes, Eric Finley, David Thomas, Jr., Sidney Raine, Joquin Holloway, and Tom Withers are friends of long standing whose commitment to the growth and development of the Mobile is remarkable. In many instances, they are the glue that keeps things moving.

In Atlanta I had the pleasure of advising, mentoring, and fellowshipping with a select group of younger Black men who are at the top of their game. They are; Marcel Henry, Kelvin Griffin and the late Charles Brazil, Paul Bryant, Monte Edwards, Devon Hudson, Kenneth Kelly, Shun Haynes, Kevin Wood, Eddie Grant, Pedro Cherry, Howard Grant, DeMarco Morgan, Jeffery Cooper, Tirrell Whittley, Nick Nelson, Duke Bradley, Otis Threet, Felker "Jay" Ward, Kelvin Tuitt, and Clyde Mize, Wayne Cooper, Kenneth Safold, Donta' Wilson. I am very proud of them with all of their accomplishments and contributions to the growth and vitality of Atlanta. You are our dream.

To Ernest and Carolyn Gibson for really helped Leteria and me come into our own, both as individuals and as a couple.

To Anthony Lee who has become an integral part of the Clemons family. Currently living in New York City, his hometown, he is a true connector, people oriented and a genuine giving person. Anthony meets no stranger and is loved by all. Glad to have him join our family.

And to my numerous nieces and nephews whom I love and adore. I am so proud of all of their achievements and accomplishments. They have become remarkable adults contributing in their own way , focusing on the mission of service to all. They are keeping our family legacy going and thriving. I am so proud to be called UNCLE by them.

Printed in the USA
CPSIA information can be obtained
at www.ICGtesting.com
LVHW021253131023
760620LV00005BA/6/J